Together Alone

A Summer in the Desert

by David Dye, MSW

Copyright 2018 by David A. Dye

The Legal Stuff:

All rights reserved. Self-published in the United States of America. No part of this book may be reproduced in any form or by any electronic or mechanical means, without permission in writing from the author, except by a reviewer who may quote brief passages for a review.

Also, the author is not responsible for any injuries, law-breaking, or harmful outcomes from any reader trying to duplicate any of the experiences mentioned or detailed in this book. Basically, don't try to blame me for any of your decisions or outcomes. Be a grown up, and be responsible for what you do, are, and become.

The Moral Stuff:

However, you, the reader, are invited to utilize the experiences outlined in here as a catapult to your own experience in nature. *We are nature-deficient.* It's as if we've divorced Her, and have a restraining order against contact with Her. Alas, there is no such thing. Get outside. And take someone with you. Then share your experience with others. Write a book. Give a presentation. Or take another trip with a parent, a sibling, a child, a grandchild. Go - alone together!

Author's Note

This book is a recounting of my experiences during the Summer of 1989 (29 years and 70 pounds ago), in the wild 'wastelands' of southern Utah. This same area that I roamed in, slept in, defecated in, ate in, and grew in, later became the Grand Staircase / Escalante National Monument. Or, at least most of it did. And since then, some it has been 'un-monumentized.'

But this isn't about the monument. It's not about the change on the land. It's about the change in my heart; the change in the hearts of those who called this land home for 9+ weeks of their life. This is a brief glimpse into the life that we lived, the primitive survival skills we learned, and the civilized relationship skills that we attempted to make into a part of who we were and are. And it's a glimpse into the three-month evolutionary journey that I found myself on. A journey that started then, and continues to this day.

Any of the *crimes* that were committed by individuals and/or programs that are herein referred to have already been reported to the state. I wrote a letter to Jan Graham, Utah Attorney General at the time, detailing some of my concerns. On my shift, there were no deaths. Later, some of the administrative players were charged with the death of a student.

But this isn't the focus of this book either. Because, even in spite of the failings of the particular program that I worked for, there is value, huge value, of therapy in the wilderness.

Some of the names, events, and other characteristics that could lead to identification of certain individuals have been altered or otherwise obscured, in order to respect the privacy of some individuals. And to protect the innocent as well as the guilty.

One last confession.

I have written this as if I'm talking with you. As if you are a friend. A friend with whom I am willing to be a bit more 'transparent,' if you will. I have come to despise the 'fakeness' that our society so much adores and values. Not that we need to flaunt our faults before others, but do we really need to pretend to be someone we aren't?

WYSIWYG (pronounced Wiss-E-Wig) used to be a fairly common term in the computer world. I took my first programming class in high school in Corvallis, Montana. I don't know if we were behind the times or not, but I know that all of our monitors except one were *not* WYSIWYG. What You See Is What You Get. We would program something into the computer, got it to look fine on the screen, but then, when printed out, it looked different. The screen and the printed product were not the same. And this, this - was frustrating.

But there was ONE screen in the class that was WYSIWYG. And this is the one we all wanted to use, of course. Because what we saw on the screen is also what printed.

Today's youth are surprised by such a thing. All screens are WYSIWYG. So, no big deal. Right?!

Well, people, as a general rule are not WYSIWYG. We're taught that it is not only OK, but preferable, to be 'fake.' And, in my opinion, this is a large cause in many of the mental health issues that we are experiencing today.

To quote Psychiatrist David Viscott, "I am telling you all this because I want to be honest about what I am going to say and I want it to be me who says it to you. I could change my style so that I would sound more respectable, more reverent, more of what you think a (counselor) should sound like; but it wouldn't be real and it wouldn't be me."

PREFACE

It was the Summer of 1989. I was 23, and a sophomore / junior at Brigham Young University. My major was psychology. I wanted to help people. But I was also intrigued by the human psyche. What made people do what they did, and think what they thought? And how could this be not only understood, but controlled? Controlled how? Controlled to help others to be happy.

Happiness wasn't something that was totally foreign to me. There were times and periods in my life when I was alive, and really happy. At the same time, there were times when I struggled with feeling that I was worth anything. It was just a year before, in 1988, that I was suicidal. Of course, it involved a girl, and a break-up. But it was also something that I had struggled with for years. Now, 30 years later, I recognize that there was also a genetic component to my mood struggles. But back then, I didn't know.

So, I was looking for a job for the Summer. I thought of selling alarm systems or going around the country spraying for bugs. That seemed to be what most of the really motivated people at BYU did during the Summer. And some made it big - into the $10,000-or-more-in-a-Summer range. But it involved sales, and I knew that if I didn't succeed, it would crush me.

I was also looking at doing what many other 'Zoobie' (BYU) students did during the Summer - work two or three jobs at fast food joints, take home the extra food at night, and live on nothing, just to save up for the next school year. I even wondered about sleeping in my car, or camping in the nearby mountains that Summer. Not a bad life, but ....

Then one day I was talking with my sister, who is a few years younger than me, and she mentioned that she had interviewed for a job with a wilderness survival program. (In order to protect the innocent AND the guilty throughout this book, I shall alter some of the names and details to a degree. This will allow the integrity of the story to be maintained whilst protecting to some degree the identity of some of the participants.) She suggested that I apply to the program as well.

Growing up in Montana, the majority of my youth was spent in the outdoors. Most of my free time in the Summer was spent camping and hiking, and when our hunting season came around, I would go to school one day of the week, and take off to the mountains, hunting deer, elk, and adventure, the other four school days (plus Saturday). Sundays were meant for Church and doing the school work that I had missed the week before.

So, when I heard about the possibility of working in a job, outdoors, I was excited. Plus, the added bonus was that I would be able to work with youth, which went right along with my desires of going into psychology.

I asked my sister how to apply, and was given the phone number of the owner of the company. I contacted him, and was invited to his home in Mapleton to make an in-person application. I drove the ten-ish miles from Provo to Mapleton, knocked on the front door of his mansion (which it really seemed to be, to this Montana country boy), and was greeted by his beautiful wife. She led me to a part of the home where the 'business' was done. If memory serves me correctly, there were about ten people in the home who were employed by this company. And all of them were busy. I met Steve, the owner, and we talked, but just briefly. He called another person over, and together we talked for a few minutes.

What were my qualifications? they asked.

I enjoyed the outdoors, and I was going into psychology. I said.

Great, they said.

And what was my experience in the outdoors? They asked.

I had spent about two weeks each year, since the time I was 12, camping and hiking.

Why did I do such a thing, they asked?

Well, it went right along with my Scouting activity.

Oh, so you were a scout! Eagle, by any chance, they asked?

Yes, I said. *Though it was on the day before my 18th birthday that I finished the requirements.*

That's wonderful, they said.

A few more questions about first aid knowledge, and I was hired on the spot.

Cool, I thought.

And then, they told me about the program.

It was a co-ed program started with the help and consultation of a professor from BYU, and utilized the skills and principles of a fellow named Larry Dean Olsen.

"Oh, him," I said. He lived in Montana for a short time, and I had met him once, as a youth. I knew that he was into outdoor survival skills, because one of my best friends in high school had been taken out on a wilderness survival course with him, and an article had been published about this trip in the Boy's Life Magazine, the official scouting magazine.

My job would take me out into the deserts of Southern Utah for three weeks at a time. Straight. They would make a way for me to go back into town for two nights during that three weeks. As a 'break.' Then, after three weeks on, I would have one week off.

Pay - $333 per week. A *Head Staff* would make $500 per week. Given my qualifications, they said, it was quite likely that I could become a *Head Staff* for at least one three-week period before the Summer ended, and if I wanted to, it would also be possible to stay on after the Summer, if I decided to do this rather than school.

I would need to provide shoes, pants, shirts, socks, and underwear. Everything else that I needed would be provided for me. Wow - the expenses were minimal, and the benefits were great. Good pay, exercise, outdoors, a chance to work with youth. What more could I ask for?

Well, one thing. I could ask for one more thing. The mountains!

I had never really been a desert boy. My life was spent amongst the pines and aspens of western Montana. In the mountains, I never wanted for water, or for shade, or even cool. And the beauty of it all!

But - the desert?! What did the desert have to offer?

I was soon to find out.

Scope of This Book

I started this book more as a memoir for my children, and to somehow expend all of the creative energy inside me that was bursting to get out. Then, as I've written it, I realized that I wanted it to be just a bit more than a poorly-written recounting of how I spent the Summer of 1989. I realized just how serious of a change I experienced, and how meaningful this has been in my life.

So, I put more thought and time into what I would write. I'm sorry to say that I am ADD enough that what you read is mostly my first draft, however. Some call it impatience. I just call it having so many projects to get done in this short lifetime that I can't haggle over a few words, commas, or quotes.

If you, the reader, would please forgive the brashness, and the irreverence of some sacred topics, as well as poor grammar - it's all pretty much how I want it.

The more I wrote, the more I realized that I wanted to recount not only the observable experiences, but also the 'inside changes' that happened, and continue to happen, as a result of my experience with therapy in the wilderness. My *alone* experience I shared with others. Though the actual program that I worked for left a lot to be desired as far as ethical and integrity issues, the fact is that simply being in a setting in the wilderness brings about it's own magical change. This is what I learned and experienced.

After I got going on this project, I expanded the scope to proportions that were both unrealistic and unwise. I was going to have an appendix listing all of the major players in the wilderness therapy field, past and present. However, there are some that have come and gone that are less than stellar, some that have come and gone that were great, and some that are around now that are amazing. I am not in the business of hurting feelings, or leaving anyone out, and given that I would inevitably leave out some great programs, and some great people, I have decided that this is a task for a separate publication. And probably more for a website, since the landscape of wilderness therapy programs, as well as primitive skills and wilderness survival, is a constantly evolving one.

I WILL include in the 'Back Matter' a list of literature related to both wilderness therapy and primitive skills. I think that this is an interesting thing for readers to be aware of. Of course, a quick Google search can bring about a list nearly as good! ;) But these will be books of which I am personally aware.

As part of this list of literature, I will include some books that are more environmentally-minded. Like Edward Abbey's *Desert Solitaire*. It has nothing to do with therapy (at least directly, though it really has very much to do with good mental health), and has very little to say about primitive skills. But, the writing is just absolutely beautiful. I find it refreshingly inspiring. And a really, really fun read. I find that, politically (or rather, anarchy-wise), I'm not always aligned with Abbey (in fact, rarely), and that I either really agree, or really disagree, with the guy. But that doesn't stop me from being enthralled with how he puts words together. Oh how I wish that I could write like him, then the picture that is in my head could better be communicated on paper.

This book is really unfinished. Every day I remember more experiences. Stuff that I didn't capture in my journals of 1989; stuff that finds it way out of the deep caverns of my memory, prompted by the small thoughts of remembering scorpion tracks on the desert sand, or collecting Moqui Marbles on Spencer Flat, or the ever-incessant wind that plagued our sanity. It's crazy how a brief ten seconds of life can be gone from memory for 29 years, and then boom, it's back again!

That's why this book is unfinished. And I'm not saying that there will be second. I rather suspect that there will not be a Volume

Two, or a revised First Edition. Too many other things to do. Besides, it's a rare occasion that subsequent volumes are as good as the first. And frankly, if this present volume is good at all, it's because of the fun characters that I had the privilege of associating with.

I would like to put some acknowledgments here, listing some specific people. But I'm not sure that they would want to be named. I wonder if I would want to be named. Suffice it to say that I acknowledge and thank:

- the students (Young Abos) who participated in the program. Most came unwillingly. Some came willingly, though they would have chosen otherwise afterwards, if given the choice. And one, one brave soul, came and paid her own way! She said that she wanted the help (therapy) as well as to learn the skills. An amazing person.

- the persons who started this program, and other programs of therapy in the wilderness. Though I did end up reporting my concerns to the Attorney General of Utah, at the end of the summer, about this particular program, I still value the intent of what the individuals were trying to do. And there is therapeutic value alone in being outdoors, in the desert, having to go back to the basics to survive. This alone is enough, often times, to bring great insight to a person.

- the individuals who read some of the early versions of my chapters, and offered feedback.

- Christine, who I met just days before I entered the field, and who, just four months after the summer ended, became my wife, life companion, and eternal SoulMate.

- Larry Dean Olsen, for writing the book *Outdoor Survival Skills*, that I nearly memorized whilst in high school.

- Doug Nelson, who taught the BYU Survival Class that I took at BYU after my Summer of '89 experience. I learned from the best. Four months too late, but still....

- Those individuals who have their BYU survival experiences in the appendix. This, for an ambitious individual, is another project to be done - collecting and putting out to the world the experiences of those who have participated in the BYU survival course over the years, since Larry Dean Olsen and Zeke Sanchez first started it in the 1960's.

- Dave Wescott, for his work at BOSS, as well as starting *Rabbitstick*. Along with Larry Dean Olsen and Doug Nelson, he's a grandfather in primitive skills.

- Brad Wade, whose primitive skills gathering *Fire to Fire*, reawakened in me that flame of love for the ancient ways that has never died. And to Enoch, Chris, Scott, Kelly, Jake, Robert, Jen, Justin, Tin Cup Chase, Ben, Pauly Lamma, Rosemary, Michael, Mindy, Jack, 'I Know Ben Homer,' David, Ed, and Artemis - all part of my 'revival experience' at *Fire to Fire*.

TABLE OF CONTENTS

FIRST DAY ON THE JOB

I didn't go into the desert to find myself. But that's what happened.

Being a therapist (now, not then), I tell people that you actually create yourself, and this you do. But sometimes a 'time out' is helpful in order to know what course you're on, and what course you want to be on. That's what my summer was for me - a time out.

I started my job as ... a job. I didn't have high hopes, or any hopes, for figuring out who I was. I thought that I knew who I was. In fact, I looked at the desert as more of a place to endure, whilst I made pretty descent money working with some bratty rich kids who lived in their self-absorbed entitled world. This is how I began my first day on the job.

Richard

He knew his stuff. Taking us on drives along the Burr Trail, he would speed up through the sandy parts, sometimes driving on the side of the road, accelerating, with his speech not breaking tempo the least bit. Sometimes pointing to a plant growing along the side of the road, telling us that this was Jimson Weed, and to stay away from it. Unless we wanted a real 'out of this world' experience, that is.

Jimson Weed

Jimson Weed, if the youth knew about it, would take them on a trip not unlike some of the trips that they had taken to get them placed into this program. But, Richard shared with us, he had known someone who had been hospitalized and nearly died from using Jimson Weed. And he had known many someones who had taken Jimson Weed only to highly regret it a few hours later.

I don't know where Richard came from, or much more about him, other than he was married to a gal whom he had met in Boulder. It was 1989. BOSS, or Boulder Outdoor Survival School, was fairly new, as an organization. According to their history on the Internet, BOSS was at this time being led, and owned, by Dave Wescott (of *Rabbitstick* renown). I don't recall meeting him, but I do recall going to a yurt-type structure, with Richard, a few times. Richard and his wife were in some way associated with BOSS, but when I knew him, he was employed by the wilderness therapy program that I was working for.

I hadn't met anyone like Richard. During my week with him, he would recite from memory facts about the rocks, the land, the plants, the animals, the bugs, and the stars. It's not that he never stopped talking; it's that whenever he talked, which was most of the time, he never stopped reciting facts.

Jimson Weed was actually just a few minutes of the hundred hours we spent together.

Buffalo Berry

He taught us about the Buffalo Berry bush, which is a part of the Russian Olive family. Growing mostly in eastern Montana and the Dakota's, there were clumps of bushes around Boulder Mountain, and along the Kaiparowits Plateau. When I was being taught, the berries were not yet on the plant, as I recall, but he taught us that the Native American's had used the berries as a flavoring in sauces, and for buffalo meat. He also taught us that parts of the plant had been used as a dye.

One other thing he taught us - that it is a thirst-inducer.

When one is hiking in the desert country, with water stops few and far between, thirst is often a companion. As long as one stayed hydrated, the thirst was purely an annoyance. And we were taught to always 'tank up' when we were near water. But the sun, heat, and wind, along with constant moving, seemed to invoke a thirst, even minutes after 'tanking up.' One day, as the three other new staff members and I were feeling this thirst, Richard suggested that we pick some leaves of the Buffalo Berry bush and chew on them. 'Don't swallow them,' he cautioned. 'They're not meant to be ingested, but simply chewed, to help with the thirst.'

All of us, anxious to be rid of our thirst, stripped a few leaves off of a bush and put them in our mouth. And whilst chewing, waited for our thirst to be gone. Five seconds - nothing. Ten seconds - nothing, except a bit of a gritty taste. Almost as if there was sand coming off of the leaves, into our mouth. Fifteen seconds, and we looked over at Richard.

There he was, leaning on the hood of the jeep, sporting a smile that would put a farting baby to shame. Seeing this, I spit the leaves out, about the same time as the other Instructor Abo trainees also did the same. And then we spit some more. And more. And more. And no matter what, it seemed that the grittiness would not leave our mouths. The more we spit, the worse it got. And then, our mouth really did become dry. And full of grit.

Each of us had a water bottle, and so we downed still another quart of water, only to feel unsatisfied and unfulfilled, hydration-wise.

Richard then proceeded to share with us the secret that we would use on our students, in a good-natured way, during the rest of the summer. Buffalo Berry bushes do not in reality quench thirst, but enhance, and even create, it. Now, unless one really does spit all of the moisture out of their body, it doesn't make a body dehydrated. But it does make it so that thirst dominates a person's thought.

This would, on future hikes, be used by each of us in a good-humored way with our students.

Milky Way on Big Spencer Flat

We were taught to read the stars at night. In the high desert country of the Boulder Mountain, and along the Big Spencer flat, where we spent most of our training nights, the night sky was unimpeded visually by man-made forms of light. The stars really do twinkle. There really is a Milky Way that can be seen by the naked eye. We were taught some basic navigation skills using the stars as a guide. Of course, I knew the North Star, the big and little dippers, and one or two planets, but mostly, the rest of what he taught was all new stuff for me. And new stuff for the others. Really, most of us had not ever taken the time to just -- look up. Most of the time we were busy looking ahead, or down. There is a whole new world of wonder above us every night, and we just let it pass by. The night sky training, and the concominent patience that it encourages, was to serve me well that summer, and even up to this day.

Sandstone

There must be seven types of sandstone. Richard taught all of them to us, but when everything was said and done, I only remembered three (Navajo, Kayenta, Wingate). These are the three major types of sandstone where we conducted the program. Navajo - white. Kayenta - red. Wingate - orange. Or at least this is my memory of these.

Sandstone - petrified sand dunes.

The basis for all things desert, sandstone started as rock, and over millions of years, was broken down into sand, and then, through either thousands of years, or immense pressure in who-knows what period of time, was 'pressed' back into rock, albeit a different form, that we know as sandstone. It serves it's purpose by being the stable base, or mostly-stable base, that all life above exists on.

But sandstone also serves another purpose. It is the canvas upon which is drawn the art of the Gods. The waves of the lines, the 'desert varnish' of the minerals deposited on the stone as water drips and percolates over and through it. The art, co-created by the Gods and man, in producing the granaries, the pit houses, the cliff dwellings, of the Ancient Ones.

Bugs

We often cringe, crinkling our nose, pursing our lips, and noticeably turning our heads, when eating bugs is mentioned. We don't have a problem taking some of the larger animal life and eating it - cows, goats, pigs, and even rabbits and chickens. But when it comes to bugs, ummmm - yuk!!!

But, even those who are vegetarian most likely eat bug parts. So this makes all of human life not vegetarian. ;)

In our 'civilized society, do you you know that there are even laws allowing a certain number of bug parts in our food?

Look this up - how many bug parts, rodent excreta, or maggots, are allowed in processed food?

The (partial) answer: 136 insect fragments are allowed in one 16-ounce jar of peanut butter. PLUS, up to four rodent hairs!

As for mouse poop, up to 13 fragments are allowed in a 24-ounce container of cornmeal. Aphids, mites, and other tiny critters - 204 per 12 ounce bag of broccoli are allowed. And maggots? Up to three are allowed, and are not uncommon, in a 28 ounce container of canned tomatoes.

These laws allowing this grow out of the simple fact that, even with our cleanliness standards, we can't get away from bugs, and bug life. It's all around us, and even IN us. Because we ingest it. It's just that, in wilderness, we do so knowingly, and not with our eyes closed.

The ants you find in rotting logs, the big ants, the ones one-half inch and longer, are actually quite tasty. Or at least their hind end is. What I was taught, and experienced, is that the south one-third of a north-bound ant tastes like a Sweet Tart. And you know - it's true. In the desert, there is no natural sweetness. Except for ants. And of their three sections of body, the last section tastes like a Sweet Tart. Of course, some imagination is required. But go a week without sugar, then taste the ant. You'll know what I'm talkin' about.

It was a delicacy to find a rotten log filled with ants. If we were hiking and came upon a rotted log filled with these large ants, it warranted a ten-minute break.

To be fair to the other two-thirds of the ant, we did sometimes use all of it. But as for me, I would crush the ant into my flour (1.5 cups was provided weekly to staff and students), to make it more nutritious, and it helped to flavor my ash cake (more on this later). In the desert, where there were no toxic bug sprays, we would use ants, grasshoppers, and other insects to supplement our nutrition, as well as enhance the taste of our food. What would be totally poison in society was food in the wilds. And good food at that.

The other insect that we would eat on a fairly regular basis were grubs. Actually, are grubs considered insects?

We would take grubs and put them near the fire, near a hot rock, not right in the coals, but close enough to have the moisture in them expand, so that they would start to expand, like a kernel of popcorn. They would die, then grow in size, and then we would eat them in their 'fluffy' state. Because it resembled popcorn, in a very imaginative manner, we would think that it tasted sort of like popcorn. A fluffy, white piece of food. Actually, it tasted nothing like popcorn, just like rattlesnake tastes nothing like chicken, but it's still what we convinced ourselves to believe.

A Long and Short Week

Richard was my trainer during the first week of employment. I was with him nearly 24/7, with three other new hires. We ate, laughed, learned, and grew together. We learned about the stars, the rocks, the plants, the Anasazi and people. Little people. Teen people. People who are taken from their soft beds, sometimes in the middle of the night, and put into a desert environment, with complete strangers, and then given the chance to examine their lives.

It was an eye-opening week. Even being an Eagle Scout, and even spending many of my Summer nights camping in the Bob Marshall Wilderness of Montana and Idaho, didn't prepare me to learn what I was learning, and would learn, over the next few months. There is camping, with gadgets and maps and modern implements, and then there is surviving, with minimal equipment brought in. This is what my Summer would be filled with.

And this is what would change my life.

A BIG PICTURE OVERVIEW

I've written about 3/4 of this book, and realize that I haven't offered a 'big picture' of what my experience was like, and my understanding of the youth's experience, in wilderness therapy. So, though this is written towards the end, it may be in the front of the book, or the back. I'm just not sure. But the point of this is to help the reader get a 'feel' for the structure of the program, and the day to day life in the high mountain desert.

Escorts

Most of the youth came to the program voluntarily. Or at least, they knew about coming ahead of leaving their home. But some were 'escorted' from their bedroom, usually in the middle of the night, by two husky (some would say huge), bouncer-type people.

Arrangements were made by the parents to hire two big guys to come to the home when the child was home, typically at 4 or 5 in the morning. The parents would often be at the front door, awake, when a van pulled up, and these two guys got out. If the program participant was a female, there would often be a female escort as well. The parents would have a bag already packed for the trip. As quietly as possible, they would all go up to the room of the sleeping child, enter it, and then turn the lights on.

The reaction was, of course, different for each child. Mostly it was surprise and anger, after the shock. Sometimes there was tears. This would usually come from the females. Very rarely was there combativeness. The combined 450+ pounds of hulk and bulk standing over the bed would discourage this.

Within minutes it would be over. The van would be on the way to the airport, and I suppose that the parents would be in bed again, but not at all sleeping.

Now, this description comes from my conversations with the youth in the program. I never did talk with any parents about this. I can imagine that the parents would be both excited and experiencing some trepidation. Excited that there really was a chance for their son or daughter to turn his or her life around. Excited to not have to worry over the next 9+ weeks, and live a somewhat 'normal' life. But also worry - did they make the right decision? Is this program really safe? What would they tell their other children? And the big question - Will this work?

As for the youth, to see two 'goons' in their room, usually wearing bandannas on their heads, talking tough, and saying that they were going away for a while - that was terrifying. Even if the child fought, verbally or physically, they would still, inside, be scared nearly to death. At least, this was their report to me.

But, in spite of this initial feeling with the program, by the time they exited my section, they would be appreciative for their parents, and the program - mostly!

Impact

Soft cushy beds. Warm rooms. Hot showers. A cool glass of water at the turn of a knob. Cold milk. Ice cream. Loud music. Friends.

Now - give all of the above up. Give it all up without saying goodbye. And trade it for: no sleeping bag, but a tarp wrapped around a wool blanket; sleeping, eating, breathing, pooping, peeing, outside, 24/7; no showers; luke-warm water; no ice cream; yapping coyotes, scurrying squirrels, and the howling wind for your music. Yes - the wind; always the wind.

No more food placed on a table in front of you, on a plate. Rather, you sit cross-legged on the ground now, to eat. If you're lucky, there will be a fallen tree to sit on. Maybe the same tree where you found grubs or the large three-section ants, both of which augment the weekly rations you are given. This tree, or the ground, where you eat your rice, lentils, oats, ash cakes, and powdered milk.

The sun and the camp fire is your light. The moon and the stars are your night lights.

No toilet seats. It's usually squatting, but sometimes, if you're lucky, you get a branch about knee height to sit on, and poop into a cat hole, dug 8-10 inches deep. Again, if you're lucky, there is Mullen around. That makes for a soft wipe. If you're not lucky, there is sandstone, spruce cones, grass of some sort, or leaves.

This - this.... is Impact.

The impact phase lasted from 3 days to two weeks, usually.

During this time, the youth would typically hike ten or more miles a day. There would be people added daily to this section of the program, because this is where the youth were 'held' until they entered the first 21-day section known as Primitive Survival. The next sections, also 21 days in length each, are known as Advanced Survival and Handcarts.

The students would, I'm told, have a physical examination. Most usually drugs were not found on their person, but many of the youth would have drugs in their person. So, this impact time was meant to help them 'come down' from being high. Water was usually not withheld during this section, from what I'm told.

There was a time or two that I would, along with another staff member, hike out to a group on Impact to 'deliver' a new student. We would be told to escort the Young Abo out to meet his new group, usually only about three or four miles distant. But for a shell-shocked teen, this was a quiet, laborious hike.

This was a time of huge adjustment for the kids. Nobody had sleeping bags. We slept in an army-issue poncho / tarp, that covered a wool blanket. All of our belongings would be wrapped up inside of this tarp, and made into a backpack during the day, to hike with. This is how it was during the Impact, Primitive Survival and Advanced Survival phases. In the Handcart phase, most items were placed inside of the handcart.

A can of peaches was given to a student, along with some food rations consisting of rice, lentils, oats, powdered milk, and white flour. After I had been employed in the program a few weeks, bullion was added to the weekly food rations. The salt, it was determined, would help a tremendous amount. And it did. It helped the cramping, the sleep, and the attitude.

During impact phase, the fires were mostly made for the students. The same was true during Primitive Survival, I'm told, although some of the students would begin to practice their bow-drill. In my section, Advanced Survival, the students were taught to make a fire using a bow-drill, and if they weren't showing progress or desire, they didn't get the benefit of a fire, either to cook on or to warm up around in the evenings. We hit the bow-drill hard.

From my brief observations of the Impact phase, I'm glad that I wasn't there. Even as a staff, it would have been hard. Just like it sounds, the experience in Impact was meant to be impactful. Tough and hard impactful.

Food-wise, they got the same food, in the same amounts. A weekly ration drop was arranged, and the youth and staff ate the same thing, or at least they were supposed to. Some staff would bring in some food from the outside, and would often use a Jolly Rancher or a butterscotch candy to solicit certain favors, or behaviors, from students. This wasn't allowed, but how could the owners of the program police it? They couldn't. Looking back, this isn't unlike life: it's unfair, but it happens.

Primitive Survival

After the Impact section, the Young Abos would go to the Primitive Survival section. They had physically 'detoxed' by then. Mentally - not so.

The emotional addictions of the youth continued on, and in some cases the embers were fanned into roaring forest fires, the longer they were away from their drugs. Drugs as in "wacky tabacky" (marijuana), LSD, Coke, alcohol, and tobacco.

Of those, alcohol is really the only drug that requires a person to withdraw physically. The rest of the drugs can basically be discontinued immediately. But don't do that with alcohol. A person can die. Thankfully, alcohol withdrawal isn't something that any of the youth struggled with. Alcohol use - yes. But withdrawal from addiction - no. But the other drugs - yup.

It is important to note a few things.

First, not all who came into the program had used drugs. The majority had, but there were some who received an education in the southern Utah desert, never having been around others who had used drugs before.

Second, this was not a detox program. The focus was not detox. Because some of the kids came into the program 'high,' they did have to come down, however. See the chapter on Detox for additional information on an alternative view of detox.

In Primitive Survival, there was ALLOT of hiking. I guess that the philosophy was that the more the system sweated, the more clean it would become. Probably some truth to it. And, hiking not only took up time, but it also exhausted a person. And an exhausted person doesn't cause problems. Sleep. That's what happened. Hiking and sleep. Not even much eating. Hiking and sleep.

I never did work in Primitive Survival. My sister, with whom I worked a section or two of Advanced Survival, worked in this section for three weeks. It was a lot more 'rough' than the other sections (except for Impact).

Advanced Survival

Advanced Survival. My home. My life. My 1989 Summer.

As the name implies, we taught a few more 'advanced' survival principles in this section. The first section was spent hiking, and wearing a person out, physically and emotionally and mentally. It was meant to be humbling. The surviving that took place was primitive. Just very basic. Nothing fancy. Just 'get by.'

In Advanced Survival we taught fire, the bow-drill fire. Trapping. Safety. And we taught looking up at the stars for direction, looking down on the ground to find bugs for food, and looking straight ahead to see others - to really see them - relationships.

We hiked less often and made base camp more often. Whereas the average mileage for Primitive Survival would be (I'm guessing here) about ten miles a day, we'd do about half of this. Rather than developing our bodies, we spend more time developing the psyche, the decision-making abilities, of the Young Abos. And ourselves.

In Advanced Survival, we purposely made life more 'cushy.' The hiking miles slowed down. We would often stay at our camps a few days rather than one. Food rations would go up. Not so much in quantity of the basics, but we would occasionally get a block of cheese, a jar of peanut butter, an occasional potato and a few carrots.

In Primitive Survival, the Young Abos dabbled in pottery. But in Advanced Survival, they actually made some pottery that was functional. Their tin cans weren't given up, as they still used them to cook in, but when a fine dining experience was desired by the youth, a bowl was used. A bowl made by the coil-method. A piece of clay was rolled out into a half-inch long 'rope,' and this was molded into shape, then fired in a fire pit.

These bowls, due to their fragility and weight, would often remain at Teepee Camp. Teepee Camp was the base camp of Advanced Survival. It was staffed by a husband and wife couple (pure gold people - so nice and soft with the Young Abos), and it was also where our section leader laid his head on his army cot.

In Advanced Survival, we started off day one by teaching the Young Abos the bow-drill. Some of them had put together a bow-drill set already, or part of one, but most of them had not. Remember, these kids weren't super motivated about life, and most especially about being in the wilderness.

So, day one a bow-drill set was put together. A descent bow-drill set. The preferred components were a yucca spindle, cottonwood fireboard, a tamarisk bow, Carmex palm rock (if one was available), and a paracord bow string. There was talk of making a bow string out of natural materials, but for me, this didn't work. I spent hours making a piece of cordage long enough to construct a bow-drill string, and it broke within minutes. Made from the leaves of the yucca, it was strong. But the forces of continuous use were too much for it. Snap! I then re-purposed the parts of the string to construct a medicine bag, that I wore throughout the Summer.

The distance that we hiked, generally, was about five miles a day. This is an average. Some days we wouldn't hike at all. Other days, we would hike ten miles. I really don't think that we ever went over 12 or so miles in a day. And that was a HUGE day. On the days that we didn't hike to another camp site, we would still hike a few miles, in search of adventure, food, or looking for good cottonwood (for our bow-drill set), yucca, or fossils.

Because there was no counselor or therapist, and because this is the field that I was going in to, I fancied myself as their 'counselor.' Teaching life lessons each day was something that I looked forward to. We would gather together in the morning, prior to hiking, and share positive thoughts, and do the same again at night. Looking back, it was a poor excuse for counseling, but I think that having the focus be more positive did help the youth some.

I enjoyed hiking when it was cool, which meant in the early morning hours, or at night. But, because some of the time our camp changed daily, we would get up about 4 AM, and hike. We would go fairly slow, and about 6 am we would stop for breakfast. A fire or two would be made, the oats cooked, ash cakes made, then we would head back out again, and hike a bit more.

We took quite a few breaks during our hiking, and wouldn't really push ourselves too much physically. At least, push ourselves by going fast. Sometimes it was just a push to get up, being constantly assaulted by the elements.

About 9 or 10 AM, we would find where our camp would be for the night, and get set up. Girls on one side of the camp, boys on the other.

One would wonder if there was physical contact, of a romantic nature, between the girls and the boys. I never did become aware of anything of this nature taking place. Even at our cleanest, we weren't 'clean.' This was a huge detractor, of course. But generally, food was on the mind of the students, not sex. I know - right?! Weird, but that's how it was.

Speaking of 'clean,' I'm sure that there was a smell about us. But after a few days, we all smelled the same, and so we stopped smelling each other. The reason I know that we smelled is because when I would go into town on my day off, I would get odd looks from others, and people would quietly distance themselves from me, if I hadn't yet showered. I didn't smell me, but they did.

And, after I had showered and got cleaned up, then went back out into the field, the stench was about more than I could stand for a few hours, until I became stenchy too!

So, after our spots were chosen, we would all gather a few armloads of firewood. One learns to do the work first, then play. Gathering firewood in the dark is less than pleasant.

The best shelters we ever had were given by Mother Earth. And sometimes they were good shelters. Caves. Overhangs. Toppled trees with the roots and earth providing shelter. At times, however, the shelter consisted only of a juniper tree. And on some rare occasions, a large sagebrush.

After our camp was set up, with designations for potty-use directions for the girls and the boys, we would settle down to work on our skills.

As mentioned, we worked primarily on building a bow-drill fire. Some youth could pick right up on this, and within just a few days, had developed the feel of it. Others spent nearly the entire three weeks working on this.

When a youth made a fire with a bow-drill, they earned a knife. This knife was a sheath knife, and rather large. It was more of a kitchen knife. Without pulling my knife out of storage, I'd say the blade was about 9 inches long.

The handle was wooden, and a hole would often be burned into the handle, and then the knife would double as a palm rock as well. The hole only went through the wood, and hit the metal of the full-tang knife, so that the spindle in a bow-drill set would have something to keep it from going all the way through. Looking back, this wasn't the safest of things we did and taught, but it worked!

Earning a knife was a HUGE accomplishment. It was as significant as having the keys to a vehicle. A key in and of itself isn't amazing, but the kind of life it opens up and makes available is amazing. A knife can prepare food, sharpen sticks for hunting, make traps, make notches in a fireboard, smooth a handdrill spindle, help to make cordage, and the list can go on and on. Earning a knife was as big of a deal as a birthday celebration, and nearly on par with Christmas!

I mentioned bugs. I didn't mention birds and snakes. We would augment our weekly rations by using bugs, birds, and snakes in our meals. The traps helped us significantly in procuring this food. And being able to stay in a camp for more than one night was also very helpful.

It seemed that most of the Young male Abos would run out of their rations about day 4 / 5, and so knowing how to get food from our environment was SO beneficial. Necessity prompted them to be especially proficient at building traps. The Figure-Four and Paiute Deadfall were the two that we utilized the most. Additionally, we would occasionally camp near cattail stands, and when we did, oh the feasts we would have! Other plants, including the Prickly Pear Cactus, were a common food.

Rabbits, though seemingly abundant, weren't allowed, due to disease, mostly tularemia, I believe.

It was our job as Advanced Survival Instructor Abos, to teach some other basic stills besides the bow-drill and traps: how to identify some basic edible plants; how to augment their diet using bugs and snakes; how to safely use a knife; how to identify and put together a safe shelter; how to find water, if needed (most water was provided at water drops); how to make cordage; and how to love life, even in hard circumstances.

During Advanced Survival, most of the crude spoons from the Primitive Survival days were burned, because of the newly acquired knife. With this knife, along with coals from the fire and sandstone (used as sandpaper), a smooth, splinter-free, well-shaped spoon could be made. I smile now to think back on how a nice spoon added to the eating enjoyment at mealtimes.

The first spoons, used in Primitive Survival, would be simple sticks, smoothed out by rubbing them along sandstone, to create a somewhat flat surface. I think of those two-inch wooden spoons that I used to get as a child when we went on field trips to the Meadow Gold

Ice Cream plant. Flat wood. But the kids spoons were more like 8 inches long.

But after getting a knife, a really nice spoon could be made. If we were near cottonwood, this softer wood was easier to work with. And we would make a point to go by cottonwoods occasionally, as these made great fireboards for the bow-drill sets we carried. But some Abos, including myself, like the feel of a little more 'sturdy' wood, so we used juniper. A bit harder to work with initially, it also left a sort of aftertaste for the first little while. But soon this wood would take on it's own shiny brown color, and became not only a functional tool, but a work of art.

So, the afternoons were spent constructing bow-drill sets, identifying plants, making cordage for the Paiute Deadfall trap, carving the sticks for this and the Figure Four trap, some chipping of agate and jasper, and practice, practice, practice bustin' a coal!

During the month of May and early June, the nights were chilly. And in preparation for some of the cold nights, the Instructor Abos were taught, and passed along to the Student Abos, how to make a coal bed. We would dig a hole about 15 inches deep, put some rocks in the hole, and build a fire on the rocks. The fire would heat the rocks up, and when the fire itself died down, and left just coals, we would bury these coals and rocks with the soil we had removed. Within a short time, the heat would rise through the earth, and make the person sleeping on top toasty warm.

Because our environment was so dry, we didn't have to worry about getting 'water logged' rocks. You see, a rock with moisture in it could be deadly. Apply heat to this rock, the water would expand into steam, and there would soon be enough pressure to 'explode' the rock. But as I mentioned, this wasn't too much of a concern.

However, one night in particular, as I was sleeping, I was awakened by the earth moving. Something below me had 'popped' just like a popcorn kernel. I woke up just in time to consciously feel a second rock pop underground. Apparently, the rocks had moisture in them, and had heated enough to explode. But that was OK. Because there was about 12 inches of soil between those 'rock bombs' and me. Little things like this made our excitement.

There were some very conflicting opinions about building a coal bed, and in the end, the 'environmentalists' won the debate. It was said that the soil that was placed on top of the hot rocks and coals became sterile, and this would prevent plants from growing on it. This was the primary concern voiced. After debate at higher pay grades than where I was, it was decided that we would no longer teach or practice the 'coal bed method' of staying warm at night. That made for some sleepless times after this.

(As a matter of note, I've since made a coal bed three or four times whilst out camping, and when visiting the same sites a few years later, I have seen plants growing over the old coal bed spot. So, although there may be other reasons to not build a coal bed, sterilizing the soil is one that I'm convinced is erroneous.)

Handcarts

After spending 21 days in Advanced Survival, the Young Abos graduated into Handcarts. This, too, was a 21-day section. From what I've heard, this section was actually the most boring of the sections. But it was not the least-liked section. The least-liked time was Impact.

In Handcarts, the Young Abos would hike ALOT. There was about 175 miles of hiking, with handcarts, along the *Hole in the Rock road*, and some side roads, during this section. And this didn't count the hiking that took place as day-hikes, without the handcarts. BUT, the youth would carry their belongings in a handcart. Typically there were four to six students per handcart, and all day long they would push and pull, through the hot sun, over the road, sometimes being passed by vehicles.

Their final destination - the Colorado River and Lake Powell.

They would get to THE section known as the *Hole in the Rock*. This is where early Mormon Pioneers built a road into the side of a mountain. The didn't chip the mountain away, but rather drilled holes into the mountain, placed timbers into these holes, then lowered their wagons down the cliff, to the land below. Down to the Colorado River, the lifeblood of the desert.

Eventually, of course, a dam would be constructed, which would back up the river, and Lake Powell would form. But for the early pioneers, it was just the river. For the youth in the program, it was adventure, water, bathing, and respite from the heat.

Their food consisted of more elaborate meals, and much more variety. They would cook in Dutch Ovens during some of their more extended available times, and dined in luxury (relatively speaking). I understand that they rotated the chores of the camp, but eventually the good cooks were discovered, and were kept. In that world, like in the cowboy days of 150 years prior, a good Chuck wagon Master was highly sought after. And you didn't want to make the cook mad, or your portion was smaller, or the scraped burnt edges!

Looking back, I wish that I had asked to work in each section of the program. Just for the experience. On one of my days off, I drove to Lake Powell via *Hole in the Rock road,* and saw a group of kids. It was fun to see them, and to experience the drive and seeing Lake Powell.

Run-In / Graduation

This was not actually a separate section of the program, but the last three-ish days of the entire program.

A Young Abo would spend at least 63 days in the program, though it ended up being more than this by a few days, or even more. If behavioral issues persisted whilst in the program, the youth would stay in the program for an extra few days to few weeks.

But no matter how long he was in the program, the last three days were saved as a Run-in. This is where the kids were given clean clothes (not new - just washed), scrubbed from top to bottom, some had a hair cut, and were set up in a new camp, a clean camp, and met their parents.

What happened, from what I've been told, is that parents flew out to Utah, and were taken out into the 'field.' They were given tents to sleep in, and a totally different meal than their children had been given the last 9+ weeks. They spent some time, just hours I believe, with some of the program administrators, being educated on what their children had gone through during the past nine weeks, and how to maximize good behavior once the youth and family were reunited.

Then, the youth would 'run in' to their parents. The kids had camped about two miles away from the adult (run in) camp, and when given the word, would 'run' to their parent's camp.

I did not ever observe this, though I was told, and can imagine, that it was a joyous occasion. Absence makes the heart grow fonder, so the saying goes. And from the descriptions given to me, the youth were in a good way when they saw their parents for the first time in over two months. And the parents were reservedly excited to see their child.

Usually, the last interactions had been very negative, and especially when the youth realized that they were being sent to a 'camp.' So, the parents wondered, would their children yell, punch, and curse, or would they - actually have changed? And the youth wondered if their parents would see them in a different light, and come to accept their new-found appreciation for their family, good friends, and food?

Nearly 100% of the time, change is what happened. If it wasn't going to happen the parents would have been forewarned.

Softness prevailed. Tears flowed. Hugs abounded.

And then the Young Abos had a feast. At least to them.

Dutch oven dinners, food with sugar in it. Real cups and plates, and a place to sit when eating. All of it was -- different.

The next few days the parents were then taught by their child how to make a bow-drill fire, how to make ash cakes, using bugs to provide better nutrition (yup - it did happen). The parents were taught by their Young Abo how to sleep in a tarp and blanket, and how to listen to and observe the sounds of the desert. To look up, down and across, and to value all of the ways of looking.

Overall, the run-in was a great experience.

PEACHES

It was her first day away from home. Actually, her first few hours away from home. She still smelled, um..., civilized. Her face was a bit tear-streaked, but other than this, her clothes, her shoes, her demeanor, seemed quite out of place.

Her clothes were all so pressed and even and good-smelling. Even though she had changed into the clothes her parents had sent with her - hiking boots (the best high-end brand), cotton hiking pants, a plain t-shirt with a really fancy jacket covering it, designer socks, and her head with no hair out of place, she still didn't quite fit in. But, I knew that this would change. But not for a day or two!

When a Young Abo came into the program, after everything in town was done (a physical, checked for contraband, their 'outdoor clothes' issued, and their equipment given to them), they were brought out into the field. It didn't matter if it was early in the morning or late at night, the Young Abos came out whenever they were ready. Sometimes two or three students came out together, and a bigger 'ceremony' was put on.

But today, it was only her. And as part of her belongings for the next 9+ weeks of her life, she was given a can of peaches. Coming, as she did, from a wealthy home where a maid was a part of her life, it is doubtful that she had even seen a can of peaches before. She was probably one of those kids who thought that milk really came from a supermarket, and didn't know that it came from the underside, and inside, of a bovine.

The can of peaches, to those other six students in the program, made them drool. For some, it had only been a few days since they received their can of peaches. But for others, it had been nearly two weeks, and just the sight of that can of peaches made their mouth water like never before.

And all of the Young Abos knew what she, the new student, was thinking, and were anxiously watching her to see what she would do.

She didn't disappoint!

One of the staff members stepped up with his *P-51*, and offered to open the can for her. This can, she was told, would be vital to her for the next three weeks. Each of the three sessions of the program lasted three weeks, minimum. And during this three week period, the can, called a 'billy can,' would be her cooking container, her eating container, and her cup. It would also, on occasion, serve to dig a cat hole, or to dig up roots for eating. The can gave *Multi-Purpose* a new meaning.

All she could do was stare, with her mouth a little open, not saying a word. As she listened, she even stopped breathing for a few seconds. Holding her breath. Not sure if he was giving her the straight scoop, or pulling her leg. Eating and digging with the can. For three weeks? Really!

I'm sure that she was wondering how in the world she had ended up going from her cushy, music-filled, private bedroom life in the upper-class area back East, to the deserts of southern Utah, in less than 24 hours. But I really don't know what she was thinking, because she wasn't saying a word. In fact, she continued to STOP breathing. Not like the passing out stopping-breathing, but the shocked kind of stopping-breathing.

When she finally spoke, she said something to this effect.

"So, I'm really expected to eat this stuff!"

It wasn't a question, but rather an exclamation.

As I looked at the group of six students, all staring at their new soon-to-be group-mate, they each had their eyes locked on her, with their mouths open. A few, without even knowing it, ever so slightly shook their heads 'yes.' Of course you eat the peaches. Who wouldn't?

But then again, they all knew the answer, because they had all been in this same position not too long before.

And there was silence.

Finally, a staff member, with an ever-so-slight smile, spoke up. "Yes. You're welcome to eat the peaches, but nobody is going to make you eat them. But I'll tell you this; if you don't eat them, there are any number of people here who will eat them in a New York minute."

The Young Abo just looked at him, then back to the can of peaches. After a second, she slowly handed the unopened can of peaches to the staff member who had offered to open them. He took the can, readied his *P-51*, and began to make his way around the can, with the juices coming out of the cut he was making at the top of the can.

At this point, even my mouth was watering. I could almost taste the juice, and even though I knew that it was warm, from the desert heat, I also knew that it would be sweet. Even for me, it had been a week since I had anything with sugar in it, and I was as crazy hungry for sweet stuff as the students were. Or almost as hungry.

A *P-51*, for those who don't know, is the military can opener. In the program, we were issued a *P-51*, to use instead of our knives, to open cans. We, meaning the Instructor Abos. It was rare that we had any food in a can, but when we did, we used the *P-51* to open the can. A sharp knife was a necessity, and using a knife to open a can, though it works, dulls the edge severely.

When he had opened about 3/4 of the can, or a bit more, he handed it back to her. Through experience, it was found that leaving part of the lid attached to the can was very helpful, as a handle. Some had made the mistake of taking the lid all of the way off, and regretted it for the next 3+ weeks.

Well, *Little Miss New Student* (I'm smiling as I type this, with no hard feelings at all) decided that the sight of those peaches inside the can were just not appealing to her. She had opened the lid, looked in, sniffed, and literally turned up her nose. Then she looked over her can to the students she was about to join, and saw them all staring at her, just looking. But not really at her, but at the peaches. At the peaches, and at her. Just staring.

She let out a little snort of a laugh, and then, as some anticipated, she started to dump those peaches out, onto the ground! Oh, and when she did, there was a universal movement from the group of students. They all moved forward, just half a step, and didn't take their eyes off of the peaches.

She heard them move, and probably saw their movement, and stopped pouring the peaches out. Only a trickle of juice had gone to the ground, and with as sandy as it was, had already soaked into the ground. But there was still a wet spot on the ground, and this - this - is what had the attention of the students. As soon as she poured those peaches out, and that juice out, they were no longer her peaches, but they were up for grabs!

In the groups, there was no designated 'leader' amongst the students. But there is always a leader, or someone who emerges as the leader. It just seems to be a personality thing. And so it was in this group. The 'leader' in the group was a male, and as soon as the Young Abo stopped pouring, and looked at her new group, this leader stood up straight, and whilst still looking at the Young Abo with the can of peaches, directed his comments towards his fellow Young Abos.

"OK, so, we're going to do this fair." As he spoke, he drew a line in the sand in front of the group.

"Everyone stand behind this line. Don't go until Bending Bow tells us to go. Then, whatever she dumps out, is free game."

Priscella (we'll call the new student this), just stood looking at the group, and slowly the realization of what the group leader said started to settle in with her. The look on her face showed the shock of her realization, as it came to her. These kids were going to race for her peaches, or the peaches she dumped onto the ground And they were - going to eat them! Really!?

Disgust.

It showed on her face.

But for a second, something else came onto her face. Questioning. Was she really sure that she didn't want these peaches?

But all it took was one more look and sniff downward, and she knew. No -- she had never eaten canned peaches before (at least not that she was aware of), and wasn't about to start now.

So, having made up her mind, she then proceeded to slowly turn her can sideways, and the contents began to fall to the ground. First some juice, then a peach, then a clump of peaches, and then it was over. For good measure, she even shook her can upside down a few times, to rid it of as much remaining juice as she could.

Then, she threw her can. For her uninitiated arm, it wasn't really a bad throw. But still, it only went about 15 yards before hitting a rabbit brush bush, then came to a rest on the ground near the bush.

She looked back at the group of students just as Ed (we'll call the leader Ed) hurriedly instructed the students to all stand behind the line, and get ready to run. They weren't far away, and it wasn't going to be a long race. But every second counted, as the juice was soaking into the ground. The peaches, full of fructose, were coveted, but the juice, sweetened with sucrose, was the most tempting thing. And every second that they waited was a second more that it sunk into the ground.

Ed looked at Bending Bow, waiting for the word to go, and so did everyone else. Bending Bow, seeing the looks coming towards him, relished this moment. He looked back at the group, and was tempted to wait a few more seconds, but then he saw the look in their eyes, and knew that three more seconds was more than some of them would wait, and then chaos would ensue. So, as soon as he could take a breath, he yelped , 'GO!'

The jump couldn't have been coordinated any better. As if one, the group of Young Abos lunged away from the line, towards the warm, dirty peaches, and the juice-soaked soil underneath them. Ed, being one of the largest youth in the group, was at the peaches within three bounds, and as he dived towards the pile of peaches, he dove straight towards Priscella's feet. Not so much towards her feet, but towards the ground where her feet were, which was just inches away from the peaches.

In one of her first moments of good decision-making within the last 24-hours, she decided to step back, away from the peaches. She was so shocked initially, that she hadn't moved. But seeing a 150 pound youth coming her direction, at knee level, caused her shocked state to take a back seat to her desire for self-preservation. As I think about it now, it may not even have been a conscious decision on her part, as much as her lizard brain (I thank Seth Godin for this term), that caused her to move.

Ed still ended up clipping her shins, but without moving, the consequences would have been much worse. As it was, Ed's 150 pounds was no match for the cumulative weight of the other five youth, who also bumped into him. When the dust settled, or rather, when the bodies settled, Ed, though first on scene, had been bumped to be one of the furthest away. Bummer for him. But in this dog-eat-dog world, first place doesn't always mean winner. The early bird doesn't always get the worm!

Literally, within ten seconds there wasn't a peach left (everyone, including Ed, got at least one slice of peach). And the soaked ground beneath the peaches? Gone too. All of it.

As Matt Graham writes about in his book *Epic Adventure*, the wilds don't have many bacteria to cause illness. It is civilization that is the breeding grounds for disease and sickness. So, eating the sucrose-soaked soil wasn't a concern for me, or for the students, or for any of us out there. The sweet savory soil was oh so worth it! And within a few days, the unused stuff would come out the hind end, into a cat hole, to be recycled. It was all quite natural, really.

At least, it was all quite natural to those of us who had been out there for over a week. To poor Priscella, our *Little Miss New Student,* it was nearly nauseating. She didn't have words to describe what she had just witnessed. She had grunts. She had silence. But, she had no words.

With the fun over, Ed picked himself up off the ground, dusted himself off, then went over to the rabbit brush bush, and picked up Priscella's can. Without fanfare, he bent her lid into a usable form to put through the paracord holding her survival pack together (comprised of a tarp, wool blanket, paracord, and a very few personal items), and handed her the can. As he did so, he said, "Thank you."

Priscella just looked at him. A blank look. Then she took the can. And still looked. Not a word. Just looked. She didn't say a word - just looked. And Ed looked back, and then, just as it was getting a bit uncomfortable, Ed turned away. Priscella - she just continued to look at Ed. After ten or so seconds, she slowly looked at her can, mouth still open, then turned to place it near her survival pack.

BUSTIN' A COAL

Happy Sage jumped up and down, screaming and hollering, holding her tinder bundle 'bird's nest' in her hands. It was her first fire with a bow-drill. After weeks of trying, crying, and perspiring, she had 'busted a coal.' She was about to 'graduate' into the third section of the program, so she had been outdoors for over six weeks. Nearly three of those weeks had been with me, in Advanced Survival. She'd gone through Primitive Survival, the first three weeks of the program, and had learned to make cordage, knot, make some traps, and make a basic survival shelter. She'd searched for and found water in deeply shaded canyons, near cottonwood trees (by digging), and in natural bowls in rocks, after a rainstorm. She had learned what it was to hike one mile more, after hiking three in very rough country. Then to hike another mile. Then another, up to ten miles a day, when three was where she was going to collapse.

But the biggest hurdle that she had finally overcome, was to 'bust a coal.'

And as she jumped, she made a figure eight in front of her, using the wind of the motion of her hands to give life (oxygen) to the fuel (tinder bundle) and the heat (coal). And, after a few figure eights, wa-la - flame! And, silly girl, she forgot to let the tinder bundle go. Or maybe she remembered, but just didn't want to let it go -- this moment was almost magical. But, a few singed arm-hairs later, she finally dropped her flaming tinder bundle, still with a huge smile on her face.

Because it wasn't yet dinner time, there was no need for a fire, and especially in the desert heat of July. So, when flame was born, it was 'the rule' that after a staff member saw it, the tinder bundle was stomped on, to put the flame out. Even in the desert, there are places that a wildfire could start. And this was one of those places. It was a high-desert juniper forest, and the earth was sandy, but also covered with centuries of rotted and rotting juniper leaves, bark, and wood. And clumps of grass, growing all around.

Happy Sage, still smiling from ear to ear, even with singed hairs on her right arm, stood admiring the dancing flame at her feet. And all the while, the dancing flame, growing from this admiration, started to spread beyond the borders of the tinder bundle. But as the flame creeped away from the tinder bundle home, another Young Abo took matters into his own hand and stomped on the tinder bundle, and with a few flicks of his foot, the flame was gone. A few drops of water later, even the heat was gone, with just a few chared pieces of Juniper bark to show for the three-week accomplishment that had just taken place.

In the bush, fire was a necessity. In my lifestyle today, and especially as I write this, there are forests on fire throughout the west. Lives have been lost in California. Hundreds of thousands of acres have been lost to fire. Actually, the scarred acreage is still there. But the animal life and homes, the flora, the ecosystem and the centuries-old balance, is all gone, or seriously maimed. We seem to not like fire a whole lot.

But, in the primitive world; the world of the 'abo,' fire provides life. It is heat. It is light. It is cooked food. It is emotional comfort. It is mental peace. Fire made the rattlesnake edible. It hardened the ashcakes, made of flour and crushed up bugs. It cooked our rice and lentils, and it made puffy those grubs that we found inside of rotting logs.

Fires and Knives

When a Young Abo in our section started a bow-drill fire, not only was there an internal reward, but also a physical reward, in addition to the fire itself. You see, a knife was earned when a Young Abo built a fire. And knives, the metal-blade kind, are so extremely useful and coveted. Having a knife made life so much easier.

There are six major components of a good bow-drill set: The spindle, fireboard, bow, string, palm rock, and tinder bundle. Three of these require a knife of some type. Most usually the Young Abo would borrow a knife from a counselor, or another Young Abo who had earned a knife, and use this knife to help form and shape the spindle, fireboard and bow. If a metal knife couldn't be procured, a primitive knife would be used, made from stone such as obsidian or jasper. Using a primitive knife was an experience that I quite enjoyed, as this whole summer was an adventure for me. And for those Young Abos who came to look at the program as an adventure, they appreciated the experience of chipping and using a primitive rock knife.

But all appreciation aside, using a metal knife was a much more effective and less curse-producing experience. The control one has with this more balanced, more consistent knife, makes shaping the bow and spindle almost a pleasure, and cutting out the notch in the fireboard is much easier with a metal knife.

Prior Preparation Prevents Poor Performance

Like most things in life, the more one prepares for a particular task, the easier that task will be.

If I go to class regularly at school, listen to the lessons, and read the material for the class, I will be more likely to pass the tests that are given.

If I learn to fill up my gas tank before heading on I-70 in Utah, going East, I won't stress about the 110 miles of nothing: no gas stations, no homes, no water. If I prepare my car by filling up with gas, I will do much better on my journey.

If I run a mile a day for five days, then go up a quarter of a mile for another five days, and so on, keeping this pattern, in 20 days I will have doubled the distance I run each day. In another 20 days, I will be up to three miles a day, and this is the distance of a 5K. So, after 40 days of training this way, I will be in much better shape than if I would have just tried to run a 5K without any prep work.

So it is with a bow-drill. If I spend the time getting a proper spindle and fireboard made, and find a great palm rock. Then if I make sure that the cordage I use for my string is not going break, and that my tinder bundle is made properly, if all of these things are in place, then I'm much more prepared to bust a coal.

Oh, and cutting a proper notch. So many times I either didn't cut the notch deep enough, or too deep. Either one is going to spell failure - mostly. A notch too deep, and the spindle will come out of the hole whilst it is being worked back and forth with the bow. And it won't just slip out; it comes flying out! If it hits someone, say hi to pain!

If the notch is too shallow, the dust won't collect properly. If it is black (brown dust is bad), it still won't collect together and form a coal, and the heat will just dissipate. The dust needs to collect together in order to become a cohesive glowing ember. It grows and glows by sharing it's heat with each other. A good notch will allow this to happen.

I SHOT HIM IN THE HEAD, AND KILLED HIM

Tall Aspen was a cheese-head. He came from Wisconsin.

He was, in cowboy vernacular, a 'tall drink of water.'

Like many of the youth participants in the program, Tall Aspen was a city boy. But he had a rustic look about him. Tall, ruddy-looking complexion, who was tan after just a few days in the desert. Wavy black hair, who had a rather commanding presence. Not extremely skinny, but rather basketball-athletic looking, he was over six feet tall, and could pass as fitting in quite well in the rough environment.

And he was quiet. Not that he never talked, but he was more quiet than not.

He didn't argue with the others, about anything. He would speak, and was kind, when spoken to. He treated the staff always with respect. And also the other students.

He was a worker, who had the bow-drill down just a few days after coming into the second section, Advanced Survival, which is where I worked. Most youth would take about two weeks to get the bow-drill down. Not so with Tall Aspen. He was quietly persistent, and in fact, had a fire going, a full-fledged campfire, when one of the staff noticed and inquired of him. Not being one to brag, we finally got out of Tall Aspen that he had made the fire himself.

Whenever we arrived at our camping area, there were always personal and group chores to be done. The consequences of not doing the chores soon taught the youth that doing the chores straight up were important to do on one's own, without being reminded. Tall Aspen learned this first.

So, it was quite a shock one evening, as our group sat around the fire, just talking, and sharing our stories, when Tall Aspen shared why he was in the program.

"I shot him in the head, and he died."

There was a collective catching (and holding) our breath. The Instructor Abos had wondered, amongst ourselves, why some of the Young Abos were in the program. For some youth, it wasn't too hard to figure out. But for a few, like Tall Aspen, we just couldn't figure out what he had done or said and put others through in order to warrant a nine-week plus wilderness therapy program.

So, when this kind, gentle six-footer shared with us that he had shot and killed someone, we were genuinely shocked.

A slight smile broke the usually stone-faced look of Tall Aspen, as he saw our collective shock. Then he continued.

He told us about how his parents had divorced, and how he had opted to stay with his mother, or rather, was told by a judge that such would be the case.

Apparently his mother wasn't the best judgement-maker in the world, and it seems that, as far as husbands go, she went from bad to worse.

Her new husband, or if I recall correctly, boyfriend, was neglectful and verbally abusive towards Tall Aspen, and extremely physically abusive towards her. There were days at a time, as Tall

Aspen described it, that his mother wasn't able to go to work because of the hits she had taken.

Well, one evening, in the midst of being beat, his mother cried out. Tall Aspen, not being able to take it anymore, took decisive action. He grabbed his .22 rifle, stormed into his mother's bedroom where she was with her boyfriend, put the gun to the head of the man, and pulled the trigger.

The bullet entered the man's head, but rather than exit the skull, 'bounced around' inside, basically scrambling the grey matter. There wasn't a lot of blood, but there was trauma. The trauma of the failed marriage of Tall Aspen's parents; trauma from being raised by his mother, single-handed, for a time; trauma from his mother engaging in another romantic relationship; trauma from the 'real boyfriend' coming out; psychological trauma of the verbal beatings and physical beatings; trauma from hearing his mother continually being beat; trauma from the guilt of doing nothing about it; trauma from those last viscous words from the boyfriend; then the trauma from so coolly killing him. And the trauma from not feeling traumatized by this last traumatic act.

Tall Aspen shot the boyfriend, looked at his mother, told her that it wouldn't happen anymore, then walked out after gently laying the gun down. His mother, in shock, reacted by being still. Not saying a word. Not moving. Just watching her son leave. Then looking over at her boyfriend, still barely alive, and still not moving.

Within minutes the police were at the home. Some neighbors had heard the yelling, had heard the crack of a shot, and had called the police. Again.

But this time, they would find something different than before. A dead body.

And police don't like seeing dead bodies. It's a threat to them, and rightly so, most of the time. But not this time. And they didn't know this.

They pulled their guns on Tall Aspen's mother, then found Tall Aspen, who wasn't hiding, and pulled their guns on him. Looking down the barrel at them, the police started to piece the story together.

Of course, *Juvey* (juvenile detention) was where Tall Aspen went that night, and for many nights after. He started to see a therapist, and through the course of treatment, due in part to his calm personality and demeanor, and due in part to not showing the remorse that the 'professionals' felt he should show, Tall Aspen was considered to be worthy of participation in a program that would help his eyes to open. If he would just have cried a bit more, or if he would have become angry, or if he would even have been depressed. Something besides the flat affect which he exhibited.

So, about nine months after this incident at home in a city in Wisconsin, I met Tall Aspen at his new (temporary) home in the wilderness in southern Utah.

One of the most kind and pleasant teens I have ever met, Tall Aspen shared his story with us that evening, around the campfire, and we all felt in awe that Tall Aspen was doing as well as he was.

ANCIENT ONES

"What's this?" she asked, as she held up a small piece of stone, clasped between her thumb and fore finger.

I looked up from the log on which I was sitting, and put the pencil down from writing in my journal. We were on an extended break, having started hiking a bit late that morning, about Seven. Because of our late start, we were battling not only miles, but also heat, and so we decided to sit in a shady spot for about an hour, as there wasn't a rush to get to our next campsite.

I took my journal out and was writing in it, when Red Maple came up to me, smiling as she held out her hand.

I took the stone in my hand, turned it over, held it up to the sky, and ... yup. It was a broken arrowhead.

I handed it back to her.

"That, dear girl, is an arrowhead. Broken, but an arrowhead nonetheless. Where did you find it?" I asked her.

She pointed to a spot just about 20 feet away. It was easy to spot, as there were about four other students there, sifting through the ancient chippings.

Now, being in a chipping site wasn't a very unusual occurrence. It happened about once a week. But at the same time, it never got old to be in a chipping site, either. Chipping sites meant companionship. Yes, companionship with ghosts, the past, the one's whose homes and lands we shared. And there was a connection.

But it wasn't as much the chipping site that caught my eye, as it was a weird 'rock,' an oblong rock, that caused me to get up from my spot and walk to it. Beyond the Young Abos about another fifteen feet, as I got closer, it looked like a bone. A HUGE bone.

It was in four pieces, about 2 to 3 feet per piece. I went to pick one up, and -- it was petrified.

It was a bone, to be sure, and the breaks in it were petrified where they broke. But it was broken prior to being petrified. Partly buried, but one would think that it was still more on top of the ground rather than buried, I was intrigued.

A closer examination of a few minutes, and with some additional help, made me conclude that this was a dinosaur bone. A ten foot long bone.

I'd never seen such a thing.

Each piece weighed over a hundred pounds, was my guess. And there was no way that I was going to even carry out one piece, given that I only had a survival pack (tarp and blanket), let alone a sturdy backpack.

I didn't even think then about the legalities of such a thing. All I thought about was coming back to get it, and the other three pieces. Never mind that we didn't have a map, I'd never been there before, and probably would never be there again. I still planned on coming back.

As I sat on the ground, on the chipping site, next to that petrified dinosaur bone, I wondered about the life that had gone before.

If the geologists were accurate, this was once an ocean, and sometime before or after this, this high desert area was once a huge tropical area, filled with palm trees, monkeys, gigantic leaves, ... and dinosaurs.

And just a few miles away, in the cliffs, were embedded shark's teeth.

On top of this, we were sitting on an ancient chipping site. How ancient, I didn't know. I presume that it was not as old as the bone in front of me. Maybe the Anasazi, or Fremont, or whatever tribe it was, had used part of the petrified bone to make a spear head or arrow head?!

We were, I began to feel, on sacred ground. Ground that had, over the millions of years, seen countless civilizations, or forms of life, come and go. Human. Animal. Insect, Plant. All of it, come and go. Flourish, then vanish. Some made this home. Others, like us, left our mark of just a few minutes habitation, then on to other parts of our life.

Shaken from my ponderings by some verbal scuffles from the some of the Young Abos, I stood up and called our little group to order. After pausing for a few brief moments to see if anyone else could feel the sense of Spirit here that I did (only one volunteered that she did, that I recall), we left.

And a part of me is still there, on Death Ridge, sitting on the chipping site, next to that petrified dinosaur bone, unwilling to leave.

Why unwilling to leave, I wonder?

Because I value what I felt there, and some part of me wants to be a part of it. To be a part of it when it all comes together again. When the Native Abos who chipped there return, and the dino returns, the palms return. I want to be there, to be accepted as a part of them, a part of that spot.

ADAPT, IMPROVISE, AND OVERCOME

"We cannot control the wind, but we can direct the sail."
Author Unknown

"What do you have there?" I asked, as she pulled her bow-drill set from her pack.

"It's my bow-drill," she responded.

As if I didn't have eyes!

"Ya, it is. But, WHAT is that white thing?"

She looked at me, smiled, looked at the 'white thing' in her right hand, then looked back at me.

"It's my palm rock," she retorted.

"Uh huh," I said, twisting my mouth into a wry smile. "Sure looks like a rock to me."

It looked nothing like a rock, actually. White, shiny, smooth in a tubular sort of way. And far too 'perfect' to have come from nature. You will find spheres in nature, but rarely will you find something that can be mirrored, and was the same dimensions all the way around. Nature just doesn't look that way. 'Perfect' in nature is not the same as 'perfect' in civilization.

She saw my smile, and smiled back. Then she handed me the object.

I took in in my hand and eyed it closely. And then, I saw it. It was an empty Carmex container.

Back in the 1980's, Carmex containers were glass jars, and for a bow-drill set, nothing could be better! This I was taught during the Summer of 1989. It wasn't 'Abo,' but it was great!

One of the primary purposes of the palm rock is to allow the spindle to turn without creating friction. We would go through all sorts of maneuvers to make this happen - spin the spindle between our nose and cheek, in order to collect the oils from our face; pick our ear wax out and rub it on the palm-rock side of the spindle, using the wax as a friction-reducer; use fat from the animals that we killed, as a lubricant; and any other number of ways to reduce the friction.

Many of us would use a smoothed-out river rock, that was large enough for our hand, but not too large, and had an indentation on the underside, usually of our making that was smooth, where the spindle could find a 'home' with little effort. Or we would find a bone from an animal that had died, and use this. the joint from a femur seemed to work well, and some of the students used a backbone. If the animal had been dead too long, and the bones were weathered, they didn't work as well. Or a piece of juniper.

But this -- the Carmex jar -- worked the best.

Someone had discarded this jar near an old campfire spot, and this student had picked it up, adapted it's use, and came up with a great idea. Soon, the staff would be saving their Carmex jars and giving them to students to use as a palm rock. This, in addition to a hole in the handle of the knives, were what was used the most as palm 'rocks' in making a bow-drill fire.

The first few years after I came back from working in the program, I would take two and three-day wilderness trips. And a month or two before each trip, I'd get a jar of Carmex, use it on my lips (as a gift to my wife ;)), then use the jar as part of my bow-drill set. However, in the mid-90's, I noticed that the glass turned to plastic, and that the plastic didn't work. Talk about bummed out!

Now, 29 years later, as I write this, I thought to myself, "What ever happened to the glass Carmex jars?" So, as most people do today, when looking for information, I Googled it.

What I found out, my friends, is the rest of the story, and a good example of how the Carmex company also adapts, improvises, and overcomes! This is a letter from the President of the company, written in response to a faithful user of Carmex, when asked about the demise of the glass jars.

Hi Brad.

Thanks for writing. When we made the switch to the plastic jars in 1996 it wasn't for economic reasons such as trying to make the product cheaper, it was because we were finding it impossible to get consistently good jars. The opal glass jars that we had been using for decades were really strong. You could drop them on a tile floor and they'd bounce. Starting in the 1990s something changed. Our best guess was that the long and expensive annealing process was changed resulting in poor quality jars. The tops would break off when we were screwing on the caps and sometimes there was razor sharp flashing where the steel jar molds separated. We were hand sorting every load of jars and tossing up to half of every load. I was getting letters from customers telling us about how they had cut themselves trying to open their jars. We finally realized that the only practical solution was to have jars made in solid plastic so that they would look and feel as much as possible like the familiar glass ones. To be honest, our profit margin did go up after the switch because the plastic jars cost us less to purchase. And because they weigh less, we saved on shipping costs, too. What we did rather than reduce the selling price was to maintain the selling price for a longer period as our costs of the other components increased (caps, ingredients, labor, etc.) and pass the savings onto our customers over time.

The look of our jars has recently undergone a couple of changes. Our purchasing manager Jim is pointed out that we had 20% extra plastic in the bottoms of the jars than was functionally necessary so we removed the excess material while maintaining the familiar height and look of the original jars. That said - the amount of product you receive is still .25 ounce, the exact same amount as when my grandfather first created and hand poured jars in 1937 despite the bigger cavity on the outside bottom of the jars. If you visit our website there is a technical drawing that shows how we did this if you are interested. We also added our red Carmex logo to the tops of the jars and added the word "Healing" because this is our original formula developed specifically by my grandfather to treat his own chapped lips and cold sores.

Finally, despite these cosmetic changes to the container, the formula remains the same.

I used to offer to send people a free glass jar when I received letter such as your's but unfortunately we finally ran out of all of the remaining original glass jars that I had saved about a year ago. I would however be happy to send you a new jar or sample of something else if you'd like. If so, please mail me a note reminding me about this exchange along with your address and I'll send some to you. My address is:

Carma Labs.

attn: Paul

9750 South Franklin Dr.

Franklin, WI 53132

Thanks for being a valued customer.

Paul Woelbing, President

Carma Labs. "

More on Adapt, Improvise, Overcome

As in life, so it is in the wilderness. We first try to control, then accept that we can't control, then embrace what it is that we can't control.

Now, this isn't always the most healthy thing to do. Within an abusive relationship, for example. We don't want to go from wanting to escape, to 'putting up with it,' to accepting that we ought to just be abused.

But in terms of what I learned in the wilderness, this concept of adapt, improvise, and overcome was extremely helpful.

I really did think, for the longest time, that I came up with this phrase myself. I thought that it was one of my most clever insights, and I thought that it was an ORIGINAL clever insight. But as with all good thoughts, nothing is new, but just recycled.

This thought isn't even that new, I've come to find out. The military has a saying very similar to this. And with the program where I worked being run by x-military, I rather suspect I heard one of them say something like this one starry night, forgot about it consciously, then adopted it as my own when I thought of it again.

Nevertheless, this concept of adapting, improvising, and overcoming has applications in life, in many ways.

In July and August, in southern Utah, there are 'monsoons.' Actually, they're usually only about half an inch or less in terms of actual water that falls, but in a dry desert, any water from the sky seems like a monsoon.

Now, hiking throughout the day is hot business. Because I enjoy comfort, I would usually get our group up about 4 AM and start our hike early, by moonlight. We would hike for an hour or so, then stop to have breakfast, then after 30 or so minutes of break, we would start hiking again. If I could avoid it, I wouldn't hike after lunch. We would get to where we were going early, set up camp in a nicer spot, then have the afternoon and evenings to work on skills, rest, or just build relationships with each other.

But, whether we were hiking or already at camp, it rained about one day of every three or four, in the afternoon. Because most of us were raised to like the rain, from indoors, we felt a bit put out when it rained on us! One could always tell the newer kids (and staff) from the more seasoned (by up to ten days) desert rats by how loud the complaints were about the rain.

A first-experiencer of the afternoon rains would howl, run for cover, glare, and maybe even curse. The rain, which none of us could control, would come down anyway, and usually fast, so that literally only a few drops came before the deluge came. And the new-comer would do everything in his or her power to keep dry. All to no avail, of course.

Those who had been out a little longer tended to just stay still, and adopt sort of an Eyore look. As if there was nothing that could be done about the rain, and so 'just put up with it.'

But those who had been out the longest, now, they were the fun ones to watch. And within a week or two, I became one of these clowns too.

When it started to rain, we would jump up and down, and do a little rain dance. That's when rain dances work best, by the way. When rain is already falling from the sky.

If we had enough time, we'd send the boys one direction and the girls another direction, around a ridge, and strip down, and revel in Mother Nature's shower.

The rains were a respite from the heat; a respite from the dry. And most of the participants, staff as well as youth, were used to showering daily. But in the desert we couldn't do this, so we took advantage of this shower, provided for us. After a good rain, the mood was higher. We felt clean. And because we didn't have mirrors, the girls weren't all of the time looking at themselves wishing their hair was different

Out of fairness, I guess that I ought to include the boys in this last statement. In fact, it was more often the males who would want to keep open their piercings, and would take a spike from the Prickly Pear cactus and put these in their ears. There were a few nose piercings, but the spikes in those didn't last long. Nor did the tongue piercings!

We learned, at our own pace, to adapt, improvise, and overcome.

When a rain came, if we had time, we would also hang out what few clothes we weren't wearing, and these would be washed too. Literally, I did see some socks that were removed from feet, and the socks stood on their own.

But, as I mentioned, if we had time to undress, we would hang our clothes out to wash, then to dry, and this was as pleasant as any machine-washed clothes ever were.

As a side note, I will state that, to my knowledge, there were never any hints of romance amongst the co-ed participants on these programs. Not that the hormones weren't raging in a big way among the boys and girls - they were. But, even with the rains cleaning us off occasionally, the dirt and grime were still a part of who we were, or who we became. I was a good two weeks getting the ring around my ankle washed off, at the end of the Summer.

To the built-in dirtiness, add a smell, an unpleasant body-odor smell, and you had a good combination to keep boys in their corners and girls in their corners. Each person learned to live with his or her own smell. But at the same time, each person could also smell the unique smell of the others. And really, it wasn't so bad. But it wasn't all roses and lavender either.

It seems to be human nature to want to be in control. And once a little control is achieved, more and more control is desired. We run, then want to ride a horse. We ride the horse, then want two horses to pull a cart. We pull a cart, then want to have a mechanical engine do the work of the horses, because we can control the engine better. Then we want it bigger, faster, easier, and on and on and on.

Look at relationships, religion, politics. Control, control, control.

But with Mother Nature, there is no controlling her. We simply - be. Just be. Be present. Be there. Be accepting. Be at peace with what she gives to us.

Sometimes, we do indeed need to improvise. Sometimes shelters are important. So we find a cave, or build a debris hut, to keep out of the weather. And we learn that we can't control Mother Nature, but we can control how we see Mother Nature. We improvise.

And then, we overcome. Those things that are within our control, we sometimes choose to control. But then again, there are some things within our control that we choose to relinquish our control over, and allow Mother Nature to continue to be in charge.

Passing an ant hill without kicking it all to pieces; walking on an established game trail rather than on the cryptogram forming in the soil; passing by an Indian chipping site because something about resting there and looking for chippings just doesn't seem right. All of these we choose to control ourselves rather than trying to control what is outside of us.

DING DONGS AND TWINKIES

Water! We didn't want to leave it, but we couldn't stay where we were. It has been two days, and tomorrow would be three. We were nearly out of food, and had just found water. By digging in a dry creek bed. Three feet down! But we were still miles away from where we were told to be. Or at least we guestimated that we were miles away. And our food, frankly, was useless, without water.

We were lost.

Two Days Before ...

She (Wandering Juniper) wouldn't hike anymore. The group had been going for about two hours so far this morning. Taking breaks, this translated to about three miles. We have about four more miles to go to reach our campsite that day.

But ... she stopped. Or rather, she didn't start again. We all stopped, and she kept staying stopped.

We had stopped for a break, and after a few minutes in the shade, in early mid-morning, when it was time to get up and move, she stayed down and didn't move.

Now, this wasn't an extremely uncommon occurrence. Not most days, but some days, there would be someone who didn't want to go on. But usually, within minutes, the group peer pressure would get someone going.

But not her. Not today.

She didn't move. The sun moved, and the the shadows moved, and she went from the shade to the sun, but still, she didn't move. And she wouldn't talk either.

An hour passed, and the group was getting very over-anxious. So was I. My patience was on the razor edge of thin.

Finally, it was decided that one of the three staff members would run to base camp, and inform the section director about what was happening.

So, the staff member started out, run-hiking to base camp. This left me and a female staff member with the group. And we moved. We went into the shade. But Wandering Juniper didn't. She just sat. Not quite catatonic, but not responding at all to any of us.

Actually, a few of the Young Abos went over to her, and physically tried to get her to stand up, but she shook them off. As they upped their efforts to get her up, she became somewhat combative, and I was worried about her getting hurt, or hurting someone else. So I called the Young Abos away from her.

And grumpy - we were all getting grumpy.

All of you grumpy, you ask? Yes. It's just that some of us kept this grump inside, rather than verbalize, or physicalize, it.

A few hours later a truck came driving up to us, or rather, near us, and out jumped the section leader, the staff who had left to get the section leader, and another female staff member, whom I didn't know.

Walking Agate came over to us, talked with us briefly, saw that things had not changed, and then went to Wandering Juniper. His voice started mild, but quickly escalated to a loud roar. Even I was starting to feel my heart race, as he spoke.

Love. Anger. Reason. Crying (from some of the Young Abos), had no impact on persuading Wandering Juniper to move. She just ... sat. Just sat, and stared. Into nothing, which is what we were surround by - nothing.

The rest of us hoped that Walking Agate, since he was being paid the big bucks, had some sort of magic that he could use to get Wandering Juniper to move. I knew that he wasn't trained in psychology, but I also knew that he had children of his own, and had worked with wayward children before. So, surely he knew some of the tricks of psychology that would make it so that we could all get on our way.

Well - he didn't know what I hoped he might.

So, when he had worked himself past the point of good reason, he gave up, and came back to us.

He said that he was going to split the group up.

He would send the other male staff and the new female staff with the bulk of the group, and told me and a female staff member named Flying Gypsum to stay with Wandering Juniper. We were to be with her until she was willing to move. He pointed off into the distance, and explained that about three 'far-sees' away, there was a road. He would be on this road daily at about 5 PM, until we met up with him.

He anticipated that this would be the next evening, though he wasn't sure.

For those who don't know, a 'far-see' (spelled various ways: farce; farr-sea; far-C; etc.) is a country term for distance. You go as far as you can see. That's one far-see. Two far-sees are when you go as far as you can see, then, at that point, you look out to see as far as you can see, then go to this new point. That's two far-sees.

So, he instructed the rest of the group on where to go, and told us that he would be back later that evening. We weren't sure what he would be coming back for, but knew that even if Wandering Juniper wanted to move in the next few hours, we were stuck until he returned.

As it turned out, we didn't need to worry about Wandering Juniper wanting to move. She just sat in the sun, like lizards and snakes, soaking it all in. But even though her skin was olive in color, she still burned, as it was an all-day ordeal.

About 6 PM, we saw a vehicle approaching. As it turned out, it was not only Walking Agate coming back, but he was bringing Kneeling Jasper with him. Kneeling Jasper was Walking Agate's boss. When they pulled up beside us, they observed that Wandering Juniper hadn't moved. It had been a rather frustrating day for all of us.

So, Kneeling Jasper got out of the truck, reached into the bed of his pickup, and pulled out three sacks of 'goodies.' Ding dongs. Twinkies. Cheetos. Doritos. Soda. For about a nano-second, I stopped breathing, with excitement. Out of the corner of my eye, I saw Wandering Juniper, and she too had began to look a little more alive.

As Kneeling Jasper emptied his pick up bed onto the ground before her, he explained that this food was for the other staff member and me to eat IN FRONT of Wandering Juniper. We were not to share.

We were to make a big deal of how good the food was. And we were to enjoy every minute of it.

Flying Gypsum, the other staff member, and I just looked at each other, thanked Kneeling Jasper and Walking Agate, and after a few more instructions on where to meet them (I asked for a map; they didn't have one), they left. But prior to leaving, they did make sure to fill up all of our water bottles. We were in a very dry area, and sometimes they would need to meet us to make sure that we had water. This was one of those places.

By this time, it was getting on to evening, and so they left, and we built a fire. Wandering Juniper, true to her stubborn self, had not moved all day. Not to go to the bathroom. Not to get in the shade. Not to tell us why she had stopped. She barely blinked.

So, Flying Gypsum and I started a fire, and started our lentils cooking.

Whilst the water was heating up, we broke into the groceries that they had brought. I pulled out a ding dong. I don't remember what Flying Gypsum had. But I do remember this. That when Kneeling Jasper broke out the food, it was obvious that he had not 'detoxed' his body like the rest of us staff.

By this I mean that, for those of us who had spent over a week in the desert, on desert rations, our body went through sugar withdrawal, and then began to get healthy. When this happened, any amount of sugar would about be too much. So, Flying Gypsum and I, who had both been out for over a week, wondered at the sugar-laden food as Kneeling Jasper brought it out of his truck.

But at the same time, addictions are a powerful thing, and sugar addiction is extremely powerful, because it's something that is around all of the time in society at large. And so, we were both excited and disappointed in our 'gift.'

But, as the water was boiling, I broke down, mouth watering, and bit into a ding dong. The first bite I savored, and oh, how good did it taste!

But the second bite was less good, and the third bite even less good than the second. By the fourth bite, my stomach had started to turn and churn. After just about three chews on the fourth bite, I walked a ways out of our camp area, and spit it out. I looked at the remaining ding dong in my hand, and took the foil wrapper off of this, then threw this out as well. Had I been smart, I would have buried it, but most of the critters in the desert that we encountered were the small pesky kind, and not the bear-size kind that I was used to in the mountains of Montana.

As I turned around, I saw Wandering Juniper looking at me, with a look of unbelief.

About once every 10-ish days, the program would try to rotate a staff member out to town, for a 24-hour break. So, staff didn't experience what the youth did - a full 63+ days in the wilderness, with a total break from civilization.

During this 24 hour period, staff would drink ice cold water (always what I missed the most), eat at restaurants, poop on a toilet, and take a warm shower (my second most missed luxury). I would also call my folks in Montana (this was pre-cellphone days).

But, the point is this - staff could, if we wanted, get a ding dong once every ten-ish days, if we wanted. Wandering Juniper, and the other Young Abos, couldn't.

So, she was just staring at me.

And then, for a ding dong, she broke her silence.

"Can I have one please?"

Soft words. Kind words. And not begging, but asking.

I looked back at her, and told her what I was told to tell her.

"Tomorrow, if you get up and hike, then you can at lunch."

She had heard these instructions, but I could see that her mouth was watering now, just like mine had been minutes before.

But, she had to sleep with this on her mind. I could sleep, having tasted it, and knowing I didn't want any more.

I noticed, though we didn't talk about it, that Flying Gypsum did the same thing as me. Wandering Juniper also noticed, but didn't ask her the same question. There was no doubt that Flying Gypsum would say no, because I had already said no.

So, by this time our water was hot, our lentils cooked, and we ate. Wandering Juniper did start communicating. She did have some rice and lentils, but she shook her head when asked if she wanted to cook them.

Small talk was made the rest of the evening, and then we retired. Wandering Juniper, right where she had set herself, and Flying Gypsum and I on opposite sides of her, to help prevent her from running. (As if running was a concern for a girl who hadn't moved all day!)

The Second Day

Well, we woke up the next morning, before sunrise, and started to break camp.

It was then that we noticed that Wandering Juniper had a half-empty water bottle. When we inquired of her, she said that she had drank it. I believed her, and still believe her.

But, she wouldn't move. She just sat. Still.

Flying Gypsum and I had, the night before, taken the 'goodies' out of camp and hidden them. Wandering Juniper, from her tracks, didn't try to find the food, but it is doubtful that she would have anyway.

Well, Flying Gypsum and I proceeded to cook our breakfast of oats and ashcakes, flavored with a bit of high desert sand and a few smashed-up bugs. We ate, and then got our packs ready to go.

We didn't have backpacks, but rather, we wrapped up what little we had in the tarp and wool blanket that we used for sleeping. We would lay the tarp and blanket out, tarp on bottom with the wool blanket on top, then fold it in thirds. After this was done, we would distribute our belongings out on what would become the inside of the pack, and rolled it up.

After the pack was rolled up, we would take about 15 feet of paracord, and wrap the pack with three wraps, and tie it off using the same knot I learned in Boy Scouts growing up, that was used by packers who used horses and mules. We would then take a 10 foot piece of belt buckle webbing and use this for shoulder straps. Not the most comfortable way to haul stuff around, but it was functional.

Well, we got our packs rolled up and ready to go, and Wandering Juniper still wouldn't budge.

Amazing! She had gone from laying down in her designated spot, to sitting up again, but this was the most movement from her in the last 24-ish hours!

Flying Gypsum and I talked with her. We kept hoping that Kneeling Jasper or Walking Agate would come along, but really, what could they do that we weren't already doing.

So, we stayed there.

Finally, about three hours after waking up, Wandering Juniper said that she had to pee. But, she still wouldn't move. Flying Gypsum, being female, was going to walk with her away from our camp, so that Wandering Juniper could relieve herself, but Wandering Juniper wouldn't move. Her bladder muscles were needing to move, but her leg muscles were willed by her to stay still.

Finally, Flying Gypsum asked Wandering Juniper if she would pee there, and Wandering Juniper said yes.

So, I left camp. After either the longest pee, or the girls just enjoy being away from me, I was called back. About 15 minutes later.

I came back to see some wet sand / dirt near Wandering Juniper, and her holding her water bottle.

Wandering Juniper took a drink from it then , with no hesitation, turned her water bottle upside down and dumped the rest of her water on the ground, very near the pee-soaked soil. Now, it was my turn to drop my mouth open and be amazed. She was too far away from me to jump to her water's rescue, so, I just stood, incredulous.

In the desert, water is a most precious, extremely precious, resource. For those of us who think that water comes from a faucet, and turn it on and leave it on without thinking, and who flush toilets with good drinking water, and who use 40-50 gallons of good, pure clean water each day showering, we don't quite understand what a cup of water is worth, in the desert.

Wandering Juniper ought to have known better, but she didn't. She didn't understand what she was doing, or the consequences that it would have on her, and the rest of us, before we saw another person.

Finally Moving

About mid-afternoon, in the heat of the day, Wandering Juniper finally told Flying Gypsum and me that she would hike. She actually just stood up, got her pack on, and said that she was ready to go. Not expecting this, Flying Gypsum and I both had to spend a few minutes collecting our belongings.

I was new enough in the program that I had been practicing my bow-drill skills. I'd already made a few dozen fires, but just like riding a bike, after you get the feel of it, it doesn't become second nature right away. And I wanted it to become second nature. So, I had to collect my fireboard, bow, spindle, and palm rock, and get this stuffed into the outside of my pack, along with a few other items, including my water bottle.

Speaking of water, I was down to about half a bottle of water, and so was Flying Gypsum, and we were about to start hiking during the hottest part of the day. I didn't look forward to doing this.

But, if it meant hiking towards the group, towards something else besides boredom from just sitting, I was willing to hike in the heat of the day. Plus, we needed water. And we wouldn't get water until we got to our rendezvous location.

We gathered up most of the three bags of goodies, which we hadn't eaten much of, and just carried these in our arms. Flying Gypsum and I carried them. We didn't want to chance Wandering Juniper eating any of it.

So, we left. We hiked. We sweated. We trudged, we faced the sun, and we went forward.

We didn't talk much for the first hour or so.

Finally, Wandering Juniper broke the silence, saying that she was thirsty. All Flying Gypsum and I could do was look at each other. After all, it was Wandering Juniper who had dumped her water out.

But, knowing how thirsty we were, we told her that when we found the next shade large enough to cover all of us, we would stop and give her a sip from each of our water bottles.

Then I proceeded to lecture her about water, and the life-force that it was, especially in the desert. I thought that I was pretty smart back then. But as I think back to that day, I was really actually stupid. Of course Wandering Juniper knew about the importance of water! She just hadn't thought ahead.

At any rate, we stopped in the shade, drank some water, which was more than I would have thought, and then decided to go on.

And as we hiked, we came to realize that what appeared to flat desert was actually a desert filled with gullies. Deep gullies. Gullies that, during flash floods, would nearly fill with water in a matter of minutes, then in a matter of a few more minutes, would be empty, except for a few wet spots and patches, and some new debris littering the bed of the stream.

Now, to walk in a straight line would have been nice, and quick.

But because of the gullies, we had to make a huge zig zag path. Many of the gullies would be about 30 feet across, and 15 to 20 feet deep in places. It wasn't merely a matter of going down the bank, into the gully, then back up again. We would have to walk anywhere from a few hundred yards to nearly a mile, on our side of the bank, until we would find a way down. Then we would need to walk sometimes the same distance, or most likely more, before finding a place to exit the gully.

After having done this about three times, having hiked I suppose ten miles, but as the crow flies only going about two miles, we decided that we needed to camp for the night. The moon was still a few hours away from coming up, but our water situation was dire, with none of us having any water at all.

Looking for Water

After we had chosen a campsite, we proceeded to look for water. Our chosen site was not fully in a dry stream bed, but partly down. We were, to be honest, more towards the base of the bed as opposed to the top of the banks. Not a very smart thing to do in desert country, where a flash flood could fill a dry gully in a matter of minutes with four feet or more of rushing water.

But, we decided that as long as we chose a spot where we could easily get out in case of a flood, it was better to be there, out of the elements a bit more than we would have been on the flat ground above.

Additionally, there were some cottonwoods growing in the area, and we knew enough to know that cottonwoods only grow where there is water.

Well, we couldn't see water, but we could see the signs of water. So, we quickly set up our camp, which meant to simply lay out our bedrolls and collect a few armloads of firewood, then we got to work hunting for water.

Flying Gypsum and I walked with Wandering Juniper along the dry creek bed, looking for a bend in the creek, cottonwoods, and sand where we could dig. We found a few promising sites, and so, with Wandering Juniper listening in, talked about which spot would be the most promising for providing water for us. Neither of us had ever found water this way before, and so we were, frankly, a bunch of novices who held the lives of all three of us in our hands.

We finally chose a site that we felt good about, and started digging.

It turned out to be fairly rocky and, after about two feet down and 20 precious minutes of digging, plus having sweated out a gallon or two of sweat (OK - so that's an exaggeration), we decided that our decision had been a bad one.

Wandering Juniper, bless her misguided heart, was also helping us to dig. But she was good for about one minute to each of our ten, because of her dehydrated and starving state.

We moved to another location, which we knew must work, or else we'd not only have a 'dry camp,' but also a dry mouth. By this time, the lack of water was playing with our thoughts, and it was hard to keep focused.

I'd read about a trick that old timers in the desert used to feel not quite so thirsty. Get a small pebble, one with edges, and put it under your tongue. This would irritate the lining of the mouth, and cause saliva to flow. This wouldn't stave off dehydration, but it would help a person to feel not quite so thirsty. I did this, and it did help.

Well, as we dug down one foot, there was no moisture. But the sand / soil here was less rocky, and so the digging was easier. We went down two feet - nothing. Our hole by this time was wide enough that we were able to all be around it, digging, filling our nails with good old southern Utah soil.

Finally, at about three feet, Flying Gypsum hit some moist soil. It wasn't overly moist, but it was enough that she made mention of it to Wandering Juniper and me. I reached my hand over to where she was digging, and dug just an inch or two deeper, and yes, the soil was cool, and moist, there.

Feeling water, no matter what condition it was in, in this situation was like getting a second wind in a race when you could all of the sudden see the finish line. With renewed vigor, all three of us feverishly began to dig even faster. As we did so, the soil became more moist.

It was sandy soil. Not so sandy that it caved in on us as we dug, but sandy enough that it was easy to feel the sand in our hands and between our fingers as we dug.

I had taken to using a digging stick, which helped to loosen up the soil, and allowed us to go a bit deeper. We were laying on our bellies, getting the sand and dirt all over us. But one would never know, since we were sort of plastered with this all the time anyway.

Another few minutes, and we had a hole that was filling in with water, seeping through the sandy soil. Talk about a victory! What a glorious sight!

Soon if was full enough that we could take our can and dip into it to get some water out. Since Wandering Juniper had gone so long with so little water, she was the first to drink. And frankly, she was near delirious. I was getting very worried about her safety, frankly, and by the minute my anger level was rising. Not at or towards her, but towards my boss, who had sent us off without proper instructions, equipment, or safety measures in place. This was just plain ludicrous. I must have had a hundred conversations with him in my mind before I actually saw him again. And none of them started out with a meek and mild sentence!

After Wandering Juniper had a half of a can full of water, Flying Gypsum then got some water and drank. A very badly needed drink!

My momma raised me to let ladies go first. And so I did. And it was OK, though by the time I was able to get a drink for myself, my mouth was so full of cotton that I could have spit a shirt out! Water never did taste so good!

We spent the next hour by that hole, taking turns drinking. The seeping in was a slow process, and it really did take an hour for all of us to get our fill of the water that we needed. We'd drink, wait, drink, wait, drink, pee, drink, wait, drink, wait, drink, pee. But oh how good it was!

After dark, when we'd had our fill, we finally headed back to camp, which was less than a quarter of a mile away. Too exhausted to build a fire, we just crashed.

Wandering Juniper did get the chance, at this time, to eat some of the goodies, but like us, her body started to reject all of the sugar, and so she had just a few more bites than we did, then gave up and went to sleep.

Day Three

So, we beat the sun up, even though she beat us to bed. We were tired, even I would say exhausted. But there was also a nervousness that each of us was feeling. We knew that today was a crucial day. We had found water, but we had to leave it! Not a fun prospect, when in the desert.

We also were worried about meeting up with Walking Agate. Were we going the right direction? How far was it? Would we be able to find the right spot? What was between that spot and where we were?

So many unanswered questions.

But, questions or not, we had to get moving.

Breaking camp took a whole two minutes. Again, no fire.

We went back to our water hole and spent the next 45ish minutes tanking up and filling our canteens. Then, with a sadness that I've only felt when leaving a family member who I really like and am not sure when I will be seeing them again, we left our water hole.

In a way, that spot retains a sacred place in my memory. That very spot was one of the closest times I've come to losing my life. Granted, it wasn't that close to being gone, but it was a harrowing experience for us. And for me, who felt responsible for the others in our group of three.

We hiked away from there, leaving the hole in the ground. I'm sure that it would be filled in during the next flash flood, that seemed to come through every week or two at that time of year. But, to fill it in just seemed - wrong.

Without going into great detail, let me just say that we hiked about seven or eight miles that day, and finally got to a road about 3:30 PM. We saw some fresh tracks, and so we assumed that they either belonged to Walking Agate, or to a rancher who frequented the place. And we had decided that the next vehicle that came along, we were going to flag them down and, if they were willing, would hitch a ride with them.

As it turned out, the next vehicle that we saw was Walking Agate. At 6:30 PM.

As he pulled up to us, he got out of his truck and, in a very unhappy voice, proceeded to tell us that we had missed the mark by about two miles!

'Walking Agate, you're freakin' killin' me man!' I thought. You missed the mark by a whole three people in the desert, without water!

In a very controlled voice, I proceeded to tell Walking Agate about our past few days. But, he didn't want to hear it. He was late for dinner, and felt put out that we were even there to pick up. And that we were in the wrong spot.

I felt that it was better to be quiet. Flying Gypsum and Wandering Juniper snuck glances at me during our trip back to the group. They knew what I was going through inside, and were just hoping that I wouldn't blow up, causing Walking Agate to kick us out and make us walk to our group.

In an extremely good example of superior self-control, I bit my lip and kept my mouth closed. Walking Agate wasn't in a mood to listen, and neither was I. I think that he sensed this, because he shut up too, and stopped telling us how much we were putting him out.

We rode in silence for about six miles, until we got to the rest of our group. He dropped us off, we guzzled the water in the barrel in the camp, and then he left.

People avoided me. I think thanks for this goes to Flying Gypsum. I think that she told the others to give me some space. The past few days were, up to that point in my life, the most stressful I had experienced. And like a wounded bear, I didn't need arms around me, but rather, space.

I went off on my own, a few hundred yards from everyone else, and just sat. Into the night. Until about midnight, I suppose. Just breathing, and looking at the stars.

Finally, my nerves calmed down, and I was able to crawl into my wool blanket and tarp, say a prayer of thanks, and go to sleep.

The ordeal was over.

CREATING A NEW IDENTITY

"I get it. I can see what my mom saw."

Whispering Pine, a previous drug-abuser (previous, only because she was in the middle of Nowhere, Utah, and drugs weren't available), sat with me as we watched the sun rise. But, it wasn't the sun that she was talking about helping her to see. It was the drug-free life that she had been living the past few weeks.

So often, freedom is sought in the name of self-incarceration. Whispering Pine, in an effort to assert her 'rights' and express her 'freedom,' had placed herself right in the middle of the prison cell of drugs. So that, what she at first controlled, then took control of her.

We've seen this story before. Millions of times, actually.

What we don't so often get the chance to see is the eye-opening experiences that come with being off of drugs long enough to realize that we're not who we thought we were. Our thinking was fuzzy. But now that it's clear, we realize two things:

1- We are better than we think we are

2- We can decide who we want to be

Thus it was, that on one of those rare mornings when we weren't on the trail when the sun came up, we greeted the sun from the top of the Kapairowits plateau. Facing east, sitting on a rock that held fossils of ancient sea life, Whispering Pine, me, and a few other students who had, on their own, gathered to greet the sun, found that in the new day, there was also new identity.

A Dark Point in the Program

"Stand still," Chipped Obsidian yelled, as the bonfire flickered in the 3 AM shadow of the moon.

"Look at me. LOOK AT ME, I SAID."

These last words, booming into the night, were meant to wake the dead, or so it seemed. And coming from a man who was scary to look at, they were even worse. Wearing a bandanna over his shaved head, with a beard and sunglasses, he yelled at the new students.

"You are here because you have problems. Problems that we are going to help you with. Problems that won't be a part of who you are when you leave this program."

"I'm going to break you down. I'll take you to the dust, and then build you back up again. You came in one person; you'll leave a different person. All you did was 'take' before you came here, but when you leave, you will know how to 'give.' Say goodbye to being leeches."

This is the army philosophy. The philosophy that this person had learned during his time in the army. This is how he was treated, and he was pleased with himself, so he would use it on others.

He would break them down and rebuild them.

Most programs are not like this. BUT, this program was. And it didn't last. A new identity is formed, but in the good programs, the change comes about from an invitation, and not from being forced.

What Really Works

My experience in this particular program showed to me that when human beings start to make the rules, and enforce their own self-contrived methods of change on others, change does occur. Miserable, ugly, change!

Humans are inconsistent, whimsical, emotional. Mother Nature is none of this. We may not always understand Her (because we don't take the time to get to know Her), but she is none of these things.

If we let Mother Nature be the change-maker, the rule -maker, the outcome will be so very different. So different. When we attempt to get in Her way of helping us to see who we really are, we get in the way of real progress. The good programs provide experiences from nature to the participants, and then stand back, and watch change come about, as if by magic.

You and I, we rebel against being controlled. And our children do the same. Why? They learned to do this, from us!

Well, with nature, we also rebel. But nature does not hear our yells, our cries, our attempts to have freedom on our terms. We have freedom, but within her boundaries. And she won't be fooled, or manipulated, by us.

And as we come to realize this, we come to know ourselves. We come to appreciate others. We come to learn and live by laws that are not fickle.

Not always, true. But, the wise one's are those who let Mother Nature do the punishing, and we simply help to interpret and bring insight into the lives of those we talk and walk with.

There has never been a better teacher than the wilderness. And the best thing that we can do is stand back, let the teaching take place, and be there to encourage when our fellow sojourners tire of the lessons. If we hang in there, we'll learn what we need to know.

The Important Stuff

It was interesting to see the evolution of a person.

All of us, staff and students, would enter the program with an identity. Always, we would bring our old identity with us. Smart or dumb. Happy or sad. Competent or a failure. Strong or weak. Leader or follower. Rich or poor. Entitled or humble. Or somewhere in between each of these.

But over time, we learned, all of us, that our genealogy is useless, when we're all children of nature, and of learning the wilderness. Having a daddy with allot of money, or a mommy with a fancy car, went nowhere in this new society. This society where what mattered is what was inside, and not what was given by birth.

As it was, those who were 'book smart' struggled in many ways. Those who were 'street smart' knew better how to get along. Those who were observant, and adapted, were those who 'made do' the best. And who made the changes needed.

Mr. Tough Guy wasn't at an advantage in a rainstorm. Or in making a bow drill fire. Sure, he could muscle down on the spindle, pressing it into the fireboard, and get smoke in a few turns. But none of this mattered if he couldn't work his bow-drill set with finesse, and create more than smoke. He needed a coal, and for this, he needed the right combination of many things.

It was the girl who watched, who practiced, who failed, who looked and learned, who kept her emotions in check, who succeeded.

When a person learned to give up who they were, and to create themselves into the person they needed to be, they succeeded.

Change a Name; Change a Person

Towards the end of our section, there was a naming ceremony. At this naming ceremony, each person, staff (who didn't already have a new name) and student, received a new name, a name that they were known by for the rest of the program.

The name was typically chosen by the head staff of the group, in consultation with the section leader, as well as the other staff. Most of the names were Native American in nature: Wandering Coyote; Growing Juniper; Longbow; Nighthawk; Whispering Rock. Each name had a meaning behind it, and each was given along with a medicine bag.

Each section was about three weeks long. The naming ceremony took place about two weeks into the section, so that the staff were able to get to know the students to some degree. Over the course of this two weeks, each student would 'reveal' himself or herself to the others. Characteristics, positive and not-so-positive, would come up. The sum-total of a person's character were taken into account in naming. But always, positive was focused on.

The name that was given is what the student was known by for the rest of the program. This name conjured up images of who the person was, and who he or she could become. The very saying of the name was also saying much about that person, both as a reminder and encouragement of who they were and would become.

DAY OFF

YES!

It was my first day off in over two weeks.

TWO WEEKS!

When I first started the job, I was told that I would be in training for a few days, then off for a few days, then back into the field for three weeks at a time, with two 24-hour periods off during that three weeks. This is what I was told.

This is what happened.

Training, cut short due to students coming into the program. So, we were pulled from the regular training program, and told to hike with the new students out to their groups. Oh, we were still being trained, but I'd classify it more as an on-the-job training.

Then, right from this into being assigned my own group.

What this meant was - no sleeping in a bed for over two weeks. Eating nothing but rice and lentils for two weeks. And withdrawing from sugar (and ice) cold turkey.

Were it not for being 20 miles from the nearest town, I would have probably quit. But I was in too much shock to think of doing anything else, and too poor to quit.

But finally, it was the day. I would get my 24 hours!

Little did I know that it would be less than 18 hours, and that I would, at the end of this 18 hours, regret having come back to civilization at all!

My first order of business was to rent a room at the Circle D Motel in town. Oh how I was looking forward to a 'real bed.' Something soft, that I didn't have to worry about sharing with scorpions, ants, snakes, or sand.

So, I went to the motel, asked for a discount (they gave 10% off to the employees and family members coming into town, who were associated with the program), and procured a room for the night.

My second order of business - take a warm shower!

In my life now, and I suspect I'm not unlike most others, I look at a shower as more of a nuisance. Rarely do I appreciate how convenient it is to have warm water caressing my body with the turn of a handle. I'm often in a hurry, and wish that I didn't have to shower.

But this day, this one particular day, I savored the warmth of the shower. I don't know how large the water heater was, but I wouldn't be surprised if I ran it out.

After what was at least 30 minutes, I got out of the shower and into some clean clothes. They were a bit dusty from sitting in my car for the previous two weeks, but they at least smelled like something other than -- me.

I threw away my old socks. Over the course of the summer, I learned that socks are disposable. I would wear a pair for a week, or ten days, then rather than try to wash them, they would be cremated. Or at least a portion of them would. The crusty nature of socks worn for ten days straight is a sight to behold. Even after the fire did it's job, I could still see parts of my socks still standing upright, because dirt doesn't burn. And it appeared that dirt had replaced part of my socks. I learned first-hand how fossils are created!

So, dressed in clean underwear, socks, pants, and a shirt, I headed for a big afternoon and night on the town! Escalante. Population -- 500-ish.

Just across the street from the Circle D was one of those hamburger joints that are often found in the small-town America. Outdoor tables only. Cute teeny-bopper girls with a perpetual smile. The zit-faced local boys falling over each other, belching as if that was impressive to the teeny-bopper girls inside. The occasional cowboy or two. A few local lumber mill workers.

This was just my kind of country. PLUS, they served just the food that I was craving.

Greasy hamburgers, where the grease made up half the weight of the burger. Thick shakes, made from real ice cream. Crispy onion rings, and thick fries. AND, Picadilly's! And to boot, they also sold candy bars. My favorite - Snickers. What could get better than this?!

Oh, just one more thing could make it better.

ICE.

Ice cold ice!

And so it was that I headed across the street, about 10 pounds lighter than I had been two weeks before, intent on gaining that ten pounds back in one day!

I placed my order, salivating the whole ten minutes it took for the order to come. All I could do was look at the others who had ordered before me, get their burgers and shakes, sit down next to me, and without even a second thought about the hell they were putting me through, ate right in front of me. How thoughtless!

OK - so this isn't really what I was thinking, but it may have been along these same lines.

Finally, my order came. But I knew better than to eat like a starved coyote after a long winter. I ate slow. I savored the first bite of burger, and then a small onion ring. This is what I had been missing for some time now, and it was worth the wait!

The ice - how good it felt on my lips, my tongue, and going down my throat. I even took a few pieces and rubbed them along my forehead. I remember some people looking at me as if I were a bit strange. But I didn't care. If they'd gone through what I just had gone through, they would be being even more weird, I thought.

And so it was that my belly was reintroduced to civilized food.

And so it was that -- my belly rebelled.

I won't go through the gory details. After about 1/4 of the hamburger and about half of the shake, with a few rings thrown in the mix, my tummy decided that this wasn't such a good idea. I was a fairly healthy person, and rarely became ill, so when I started to feel queasy, I thought that all I needed was some ice water, to settle things down. And I do think that this helped. For a minute or two.

However, the rest wasn't long-lived.

I packed up my food, and walked back across the street to lay down on the bed, hoping that this would be beneficial. Maybe a little rest on a nice, soft, comfortable queen-size mattress would help.

But alas, no such luck this direction either. No sooner had I plopped down on the bed, then I was up again, hunched over the porcelain throne. I wasn't at the point of throwing up, but the nausea was present, and went from small waves to tidal waves. It got to the point that I finally forced myself to give up the contents of my stomach, in order to get a little rest.

However, this was just a bit late in the process of digestion, I'm afraid. Some of the food had escaped into my intestines, and from there, the 'other end' of my insides took the brunt of this new attack. I thought that food took a day to makes it way through the digestive system. Not so, it seems, when something isn't wanted. So, I spent the next five or six hours lounging on the latrine. I knew enough to keep drinking water, so as to keep from dehydrating.

Later that night, when I felt able, I went to lay down in the bed again. Only to toss and turn for an hour or so. Finally, I gave this up, and moved to the floor. Within minutes, I was asleep!

Needless to say, the next morning I was anything but ready to head back out into the field. Physically, I was more exhausted than I had been in a very long time. And as luck would have it, I was picked up about six hours early. There's no rest for the weary.

And what about the Snicker's bar, you ask?

Call me dense, but on the way back out to the field, I broke into the Snickers. After about three bites, I could feel the same waves of nausea coming back. But I caught them before they grew. Rolling the window down, I threw the Snickers out.

As I saw it tumble through the dirt and sand, I realized that life as it had been was no longer. Like it or not, in many ways, I couldn't return to the same life that I had lived just a few weeks before.

(Note: On my second day off during that section, I went camping rather than go to town. The birds, the animals, the breeze, the quiet, not having to sleep with one eye open worrying about children attacking me - all of it was great.)

DETOX

From out of nowhere (seemingly) she just started pounding her fists into the dirt, crying, or more like screeching, saying that this just wasn't fair. Those who were close by her took a step or two back, but didn't seem alarmed.

I looked over, prepared to run to her aid, thinking that she may be in some sort of danger, or at least perceived danger. But a quick glance her direction showed me that those who were by her weren't reacting in a way to either 'fight or flight,' so I held my reaction in check. Rather, I stayed where I was, just being attentive.

She continued to pound the ground. Her sobs continued as well. But the intensity of her screams slowly decreased. She was not happy, and in fact, extremely frustrated. But she wasn't running, she wasn't being attacked, and she wasn't hurting anyone else. The best thing for me, and others, to do -- give her space.

This wasn't the first time that a similar behavior had occurred, and it wasn't the last. It was the most profound, noise-wise, however.

Within a matter of 30-ish seconds, the rest of us were back to getting our camp set up. All but Rocking Pine (the sobbing girl) and Straight Oak. Rocking Pine was still crying, head down, sprawled in the dirt near her bedroll. Straight Oak was standing nearby, looking sort of lost. This is when I felt that I ought to at least find out what had just happened.

I unobtrusively made my way towards both girls, who were about ten yards apart, and went up next to Straight Oak, who was looking at Rocking Pine, with a 'shell-shocked' expression on her face. I stood next to Straight Oak and asked, "So, anything that I need to know about?"

After a few moments of silence, Straight Oak said, "She told me that I needed to get her wood for her, and I said no. Now she's freakin' out."

I looked at Straight Oak. She was shocked, but she was also angry, upset, and could hardly believe that Rocking Pine had reacted in such a way.

When we arrived at our campsite, there was a procedure that we always followed. We would first locate the central fire location, then the girls would be assigned to one side of the fire and the boys to the other. Each person would then locate where they would set up their bedroll that night. If it appeared that the wind would be bad, or that it would rain, a spot would be chosen, usually in conjunction with another person, that would allow a shelter to be set up.

Then, after the location was chosen, they would lay claim to it by leaving their bedroll on the spot. But, before they started construction of their shelter, or even laying out their bedroll, each person in the camp, male and female, student and staff, was required to collect two good-sized armloads of firewood and put it near the fire circle that was made.

Well, Straight Oak and Rocking Pine had decided to build a debris shelter together. So they claimed their spot. Then, Rocking Pine told Straight Oak that she would save their spot while Straight Oak collected the firewood for both of them. Straight Oak, of course, said no way. Rocking Pine, at first not believing Straight Oak, thought that Straight Oak was kidding. But after again telling Straight Oak to get her firewood, and being told no, Rocking Pine then pitched the fit that the rest of us, and all of the animals within a mile, heard.

Being the Big-Dog

Some of the children, or really, most of them, had come from circumstances of shall we say, wealth. Some, including Rocking Pine, lived in a home where there was a maid who did all of the cleaning, cooking, laundry, etc. Rocking Pine was used to doing just what she wanted to do, and what she didn't want to do, she didn't. If it needed to be done, Rocking Pine just asked the maid to do it.

The more I got to know Rocking Pine, the more she opened up. There would be times that she would even tell the maid to do some of the tasks that she was told to do by her mother. Her father wasn't a big part of her life, though he also lived in the home. So, mom asked Rocking Pine to do something. Rocking Pine told the maid to do it. The maid did it, because even though Rocking Pine was supposed to do it, Rocking Pine would make up lies about the maid to get her into trouble if the maid didn't comply with Rocking Pine's demands. And mom, not knowing that Rocking Pine lied, always sided with her, and against the maid.

So, Rocking Pine had a nice set up. Dishonest, but cushy.

Now, out here, where she had no leverage over on anyone, she found that she couldn't manipulate. People or Mother Nature. And thus it was that we observed Rocking Pine detoxing - from her power trips!

She wasn't the only one, as I mentioned. Most of the kids out there who came from well-off homes, were high on power. They were used to getting their way. To pushing their selfish agenda's through, at the expense of those around them. And this was one of the big problems that they had to confront.

When everyone ate the same food, wore the same dirty clothes, hiked the same trails, drank from the same canteen, cooked from the same fire, stared at the same night sky, then all of the sudden, everyone was equal. There was nobody to push around. And then life, real life, not the concocted fake life of money and power, was introduced to them.

After the initial realization of this, every child that I had the opportunity to work with realized that there was a better way of being, personally as well as with others. This 'awakening' was a joy to see, and to see them sluff off their prideful power for humble helpfulness was a huge reward for me.

Within a week, Rocking Pine was much more 'awake' to real life, and by the time she left my section, she was one of the most conscientious and kind people in the group.

Detox from Sugar

It's crazy, I know, but we're addicted to sugar. You'll read about it, sometimes, on some naturopathic website, and even occasionally in the main stream media. But back in the 1980's, it was never mentioned. At least in the literature that I kept company with.

In another part of this book, talking about my day off, I go into more detail about my love-affair with sugar, and how I became really ill during one of my days off because of sugar. Suffice it to say that I've had personal experience being 'addicted' to sugar, and know what it's like to give it up. So did most of the kids in the program.

Sugar, or any type of sweetener, is not a requirement to live. When our rations were divvied out, sugar was not among them. This was grieving to most of us. But as time went on, our bodies adjusted. Truth be known, we became more healthy, and though food was what the topic of conversation was around the campfire at night, sugar didn't play into it after the first week or two. It was comfort foods, yes, like pizza, or something cold like ice cream. But for reasons other than sweetness.

About the only form of sweet that we had out in the field was the hind section of wood ants. When we came to a rotted out log, it became somewhat of a scramble to collect the ants, and bite off the hind section of the ants. It had a 'sweet tart' taste to it, and in time, became our desert. Eaten, of course, at any time of day, when we found a rotting log!

Detox from Drugs

The program was not a detox facility, and detox wasn't really even a focus. There was no way that we could have handled a participant who was coming down from a long-term, deep-seated addiction to drugs or alcohol. Or even a short-term addiction.

Don't get me wrong - many of the young participants in the program had used drugs. Pot was the most common, but there were even some who had used LSD. One girl in particular had a flashback whilst she was in the desert. Not a fun experience - for her or for the rest of us in camp with her.

Having said this, I should also remind the reader, as we were reminded daily, that a majority of the students had used some sort of drug in their past life. And most did so recently enough that when they entered the program, they were still coming 'down.' But coming down and detoxing are two different things. Or at least the severity of it.

The Young Abos would detox, but didn't come to the program with the express purpose of detoxing.

RUNNING, WITH NOWHERE TO GO

It was dusk. I looked over through the waning light, and saw Laughing Woodchip, sitting on his tarp and blanket, leaning against a cedar tree. He had a scowl on his face, which was typical of his face 90% of the time. And actually, the scowl was better than the smile that he had. Because when he was smiling, you knew that there would soon be some sort of commotion in the camp. For being so far from civilization, Laughing Woodchip still found a way to set 'bombs.'

Not real bombs, but all sorts of surprises.

One time he had set up a figure four trap in camp, and when it had been tripped, he set it up to snap some sticks, and 'fire' them towards people. And it worked. It was quite harmless, and thinking about it now, a slight smile breaks through on my face. The sticks went flying through the air, hit a few people, who let out screams of surprise, which in turn solicited other screams, and for a minute, the whole camp seemed to be in commotion. All except for Laughing Woodchip, who was off to the side, watching it all happen, smiling big!

Another time he had taken a rattlesnake skin, and made it look as life-like as he could. Which apparently was pretty life-like, as it startled a fellow male student. Now, we rather expected the girls to jump at things like snakes and mice, but the boys, well, they tended to get rocks and sticks and start beating.

But of course, being surprised is another thing totally.

So, when this fellow saw the snake decoy, near his bedroll that he was about to get in, he let out a whoop and a hollar (and probably a little pee, truth be known), and went running back. Not just backing away, but RUNNING away.

The rest of us, of course, wondered what had caused him to behave this way. After an initial investigation, assuring myself that there was no serious danger, I looked at Laughing Woodchip. Smiling Laughing Woodchip. And at this point, *laughing* Laughing Woodchip. When nobody else was laughing, this was a sure-fire give-away that Laughing Woodchip had been up to something.

Again, thinking back on this experience, some 30 years later, I smile.

But back then - it wasn't a laughing matter.

It seemed that Laughing Woodchip always had our camp in an uproar.

But the practical jokes weren't the hardest thing to deal with as far as Laughing Woodchip went. The very hardest thing was the nearly every night, Laughing Woodchip went 'missing.' He would run away.

Most of our time was spent on top of the Kapairowits Plateau. And except for some rancher's vehicles, a few really old cabins, some water troughs, and some really pot-holed dirt roads, there's nothing else that reminds a person of civilization. So basically, Laughing Woodchip would run from wilderness into wilderness. He wouldn't get far.

The first few times he ran, I got pretty worried. But when it became a nearly nightly occurrence, we would use our tracking skills, and deception to find him.

One of the staff, and usually a male student, would take off after Laughing Woodchip, following his tracks. It wasn't always easy to follow, but we didn't do horrible either. And we would make noise. A lot of it. On purpose. Our desire was to have Laughing Woodchip see and hear us coming. We would often take breaks, talking loudly, in plain sight. This was so that Laughing Woodchip would keep an eye on us. If we stopped moving, he would stop moving.

This allowed another Instructor Abo, and usually one or two Youth Abos, to sneak around in a half circle, and try to not necessarily cut Laughing Woodchip off, but to get to a hidden spot where they could look out and see movement. It really is quite easy to hide, and especially for Laughing Woodchip. He wasn't large. He blended in with the dirt, since it covered him most of the time. And he had a desire to be concealed.

So, a staff member and some students would sneak around, towards where they anticipated Laughing Woodchip would be, or near there, and then, hidden, look for movement. Stillness is the way to stay concealed. And breaking up your form; not being on the horizon.

But Laughing Woodchip, even as he became aware of our tactic, found it hard to remain concealed. Because he had to move. And thus, he would be found.

It seemed to almost become a nightly ritual. Work on skills, write in the journal, make and eat dinner, talk around the campfire, go use the cathole, and then - 'OK, who wants to go look for Laughing Woodchip tonight?'

Now, as a field staff, I had some authority, but as far as any 'program change,' this was beyond my pay scale.

But it wasn't beyond Walking Agate's pay scale.

One of the times that Walking Agate was in camp, he spoke with Laughing Woodchip. The result of that conversation was that we were instructed to, each night, take Laughing Woodchip's shoes.

Walking Agate, and the rest of us, thought that not having shoes would sufficiently discourage Laughing Woodchip from running. But, of course, this would only work for someone who gave some forethought as to what was on the desert floor. And Laughing Woodchip didn't give this any forethought. In fact, I don't even think he cared a bit -- the first night.

We had gathered around the fire, as a group, and were swapping stories, singing a bit, and talking about food, which was the topic 95% of the time, when all of the sudden we heard some screams.

This was a bit alarming. We were always alone, so any human noise came from someone who was in our group. We looked around, and lo and behold -- no Laughing Woodchip.

I've wondered, since my time with the program, if Laughing Woodchip ever joined the Special Forces. He was sneaky, and really, quite good at being sneaky. I think that if he were on my side in a war, I'd feel comfortable having his skills in my service.

But out there, Laughing Woodchip's talents were not really what was practical for him, or for us.

He had snuck away - again - without any of us knowing.

But he only went about 50 yards before he'd found, in his stocking feet, a prickly pear cactus patch. Using the crouching run / jog that I had seen him do, I could almost visualize what had happened.

Though not totally dark, it was dark enough to not be able to see the ground well. But all he was doing most of the time was avoiding cedar trees and sage brush. Plus, he would be moving forward, but looking back, part of the time, to make sure that he wasn't being followed.

Well, that's what happened.

His first foot had stepped into the cactus bunch, whilst he was looking back, but moving forward. But since his momentum was taking him forward, and because his intent was to put his next foot down in front of the first one, his second foot also came down in the prickly pear cactus.

Ouch!

A small jump was all it took to have him lose his balance, and land in the patch on his side.

The short sleeve shirt did nothing to protect his exposed arm, nor did it help to protect his side and shoulder. The cactus spines went through his shirt, and lodged in his skin.

His jeans did a somewhat better job of protecting his legs and hips. But there were still some pricks that found their way through!

This is when we heard him scream. In pain.

After the initial shock of any such event, the time when there is no movement at all, another Instructor Abo and I jumped to our feet and ran out to Laughing Woodchip, worried that some life-threatening event had occurred.

Instead, we found Laughing Woodchip, being very still and not yelling any more, with some soft sobs escaping his lips, and some of that precious internal fluid making it's way out of his eyes, half laying on this prickly landing spot.

As we approached him, my heart went out to him. It was obvious that he was in a hurting way. And frankly, I wasn't sure what the best thing to do for him was.

I knew that he had to get out, and get up, but I wasn't sure if we should gently ease him out, or just pull, fast and furious.

After some conversation, with him whispering, as if this would be less painful than talking at the normal sound level, we decided to ease him out. So, trying our best to avoid the patch ourselves, the other staff member and I began to gently pull on Laughing Woodchip.

But as we did so, his howling began again. But with renewed vigor. In the distance, some coyotes even began to respond to his howls.

So, making an executive decision, I pulled him, fast, and brought him up. I figured that if he was in pain, and was going to wail the whole time were getting him up, I'd rather shorten the length of this irritating noise.

Laughing Woodchip couldn't walk back to camp, of course, so we built a fire near where he was, and spent the next few hours working on taking the cactus spines out of him.

I don't remember ever getting a thank you for our efforts. I do remember that he started to wonder if running was the most wise course of action.

It must have been after midnight when we finally decided that enough of the spines had been removed to make further explorations unfruitful.

The big pokey's are easy to see and easy to take out.

It was the little ones, the sharp but soft spined spikes, that cause the most pain.

These grow at the base of the large, hard, spines.

They are like little bits of hair, but work their way into the skin, and really, are impossible to pull out.

We put some mud on the areas that hurt the most, and this seemed to help some, but truthfully, time is what healed this type of wound.

So, for the next few days, and nights, Laughing Woodchip was a humble person. He couldn't carry his bedroll. He struggled walking. He didn't tie his shoes up, but kept them as loose as they would go.

When he got into camp, he voluntarily gave up his shoes. No - he just took his shoes off, and then we 'kept them safe for him.'

But, pain is a short teacher. Or maybe, pain is a good teacher.

A few nights later, he decided to leave camp again, but this time, spent more time watching the ground as he left.

He also took his pants off, ripped the legs off of them, and used the legs to wrap around his feet. A few layers of denim is a pretty good way to keep spines from going into the feet.

Pretty creative, I thought. We would teach the youth to adapt, improvise and overcome. Laughing Woodchip learned this lesson well. To his detriment, yes, but also to his credit.

Walking Agate visited the camp the day after Laughing Woodchip ripped his pants. As it turned out, the hikers would get clean clothes every few weeks, and that day was it.

So, Walking Agate took the denim shorts and two legs, and left a single pair of pants.

He also left instructions to take the pants as well as the shoes away at night.

One would think that, not having shoes or pants, running in the desert, at night, would be less than desirable. But for Laughing

Woodchip, he took it as an additional challenge. And so, for the next three nights, he ran.

Again, adapting and improvising, he overcame the problems. One night he tied some cedar bark onto his feet. The next, he used a shirt that he cut in half. And lastly, he just carefully picked his way through the desert landscape.

It seemed that the constant 'cat and mouse' game would not end. And because of his mindset, Laughing Woodchip looked at this challenge like he probably looked at the challenges at home -- the world wasn't going to stop him from doing what he wanted, even if it really didn't get him anywhere.

But, as much of a ritual as it had become, one night, it abruptly ended. I don't know if we just happened to be an observer of this part of Laughing Woodchip's teen evolution, if he finally decided to pay more attention to those around him, or if it all of the sudden became a shift in values for him. But, he stopped running.

Laughing Woodchip didn't stop because of the prickly pear patch experience. He didn't stop running because he thought he was 'beaten.' He didn't stop because he didn't think he could make it. He stopped because of --- girls!

Even in situations where there isn't supposed to be a hierarchy, there usually is. There are formal hierarchies and informal hierarchies. True that in the program as well.

And three of the more popular girls got together and talked with Laughing Woodchip. They weren't asked to do this. They weren't trying to effect any sort of huge change in Laughing Woodchip. They just - asked questions.

Why did he run? What did he hope to gain from it? Where was he running to? Could he use this program to really benefit and help himself?

The end result of this conversation was this. The girls liked some things about Laughing Woodchip, and expressed this to him. His tenacity in continually running, and his reasons (or lack of reasons) for running, was not impressive to them. A life lesson from them talking from the heart, for ten minutes, did more good than all of the hours of the consequences that were imposed on him by us. He came to realize that he *did* like to be admired by the young women, and when he saw through their eyes how he appeared to them, he chose to change.

By the time he left our section, he was considered a star participant of the program!

FOOD. ALWAYS FOOD ...

"My favorite food is pizza. The kind that has cheese that comes off in strings, when you bite it and pull away. It's filled with the good stuff -- pepperoni, olives, mushrooms, sausage. That, and a cold root beer. When I get back, this is the first thing that I'm going to have."

He said this, eyes closed, salivating, whilst we sat around the campfire in the evening, after our meal.

He wasn't hungry, but he was 'starving.'

His belly was full. Or at least as full as it could be, in a perpetually food-deficient environment. Rice and lentils were the appetizer and main course, supplemented by a little snake meat, tossed in for good measure, and to add some protein and a bit of flavor. Dessert was being prepared as we spoke -- ash cakes. Flour, with a bit of water to make it pliable. This mixture was being pressed together, into a flat cake, or patty. This would then be cooked on the coals of the fire. When it began to brown, it was done. But most people charred it, to add flavor! And we had a little brown sugar this night, to pass around!

The conversation this night, like all nights, turned to food. And though everyone was different in their tastes, nobody had a shortage of the foods they missed. Hours upon hours would be spent talking about the various foods that they missed.

It's said that absence makes the heart grow fonder. When stated in relation to food, this is no less true, and possibly more so. Food was, without question, the overriding topic of conversation, day and night.

Maslow's Hierarchy

In 1943, a psychologist postulated a theory of motivation. It has become known as *Maslow's Hierarchy of Needs*. Having taken some pre-cursory psychology courses in college, I was aware of this theory, proposed by a fellow named Abraham Maslow.

In a nutshell, he theorized that there are five levels of needs that we have, as human beings. In order to move off of the first level, to the second, our first level needs must first be met. And to move from the second level to the third, our second-level needs must be met. And so, up to the fifth level of needs.

On the very bottom, the base, are physiological needs. Items such as food, water, warmth, and rest are basic to our existence. And if these needs aren't met, then we don't go up to the next levels (safety; love needs; esteem needs; self-actualization).

Each week a food packet would be given to the Young Abos. This consisted of food items such as rice, lentils, oats, cream of wheat, powdered milk, white flour and later, some bullion cubes. The amounts were the same given to each Young Abo, irregardless of body size, etc.

The Instructor Abos were also given a packet of this food as well, but we could choose how much of each item to get.

This food was packaged by us into zip lock bags. Usually one of the staff of the group would fill the bags with food.

The Young Abos were told that this was their food allotment for the coming week, and as such, protect it very well. And protect it they did. They would sleep with it, to keep others from getting at it. And around the campfire, most people kept a close eye on it, all the time.

To supplement the food, Instructor Abos would teach the youth how to make traps, and throw sticks, and chase lizards and snakes, find grubs, and identify edible plants. Almost always, we wouldn't eat the food we found all by itself. Rather, we would incorporate it into the food that was allotted to us. This way, we didn't have to try so hard to swallow the bugs. Plus, it really did add flavor to the food.

A few Young Abos in each of my groups consistently ran out of food about day four or five. That meant that they had to go two or three days without food that came from the program. During these days, they would either have what food they could harvest, or they would beg others for food. Often, the smaller Young Abos would have more food than they needed, and so the youth who wanted food would trade labor for food. Both parties benefited from this, but honestly, the biggest benefactor was the small Young Abo who had food to barter with.

It's amazing what the bigger kids would do in order to get a little food. For just one meal, they would do the person's chores until the next food drop. Or they would carry the person's bed roll until the next food drop. Or any other number of special requests.

One of the things that we didn't allow is getting out of the skills that were taught, including the bow-drill, cordage making, identifying plants, etc. This was part of the program, and this couldn't be bartered away.

So, food -- always on the mind.

Only occasionally would something else trump food. And that was water.

Most of the time water was made available to us, in plentiful supply. Either by water drops, where the water was in 55 gallon plastic barrels, or from water in the desert, at the springs or animal watering troughs. But on the rare occasion that water wasn't available, we all came to appreciate the fragile nature of our life without water. Sometimes some of us went for up to two days without food. This would never have happened without water.

As an interesting side note: I believe that over the course of the summer, my metabolism changed. During my last weeks in the wilderness, I ran out of week before I ran out of food. I would have about half of my food left when we received the next food drop.

Most often, however, I would take note of those Young Abos who weren't as fortunate as I was with metabolism, and even though we were told to not give our food to any of the Young Abos, I would. Selfishly, they slowed us down when we were hiking. And I always wanted to get to where we were heading. Unselfishly, I could see that being out of food was an extreme hardship, given the amount of physical exercise we participated in.

SOLO

I was asleep. 'Was' is the key word in this sentence.

I'd gone to the bathroom before retiring. OK - so, I really didn't go to the bathroom, because there are no bathrooms on Death Ridge, at the top of the mountain in southern Utah. But, you know what I mean.

I was asleep. Fast asleep, and feeling like it was a good night to get rested. My worries were less than usual, because all of the Young Abos were out on Solo. One night during the three week section, we dispersed the students about 400 yards apart to spend the night on their own. They had to construct their own shelter, build their own fire, and spend time meditating and writing in their journal.

It was a time when the Instructor Abos could sit around the fire, and talk about 'staff stuff.' You know, the really important stuff, besides food, which is what the 'student stuff' is that was talked about 95% of the time. The Instructor Abos could talk about life after the program, but not food life. Life as in dating, school, and showering with real, warm water, and drinking with real, ice-cold ice!

It was also a time that we could sleep soundly, and not have to worry about a Young Abo running, or getting up and stabbing us or another Abo with their knife. It was only during Solo nights and after I left the program to go back to school that I realized how much subconscious worry I had about safety.

So, I was asleep, and comfortably so, when all of the sudden I was awakened by screaming that was in camp, right near where my fire used to be.

Had my bladder not been empty, it would soon have emptied!

I jumped up and, ending in a defensive pose, ready to beat off the pack of wolves that had entered our camp, all I saw was Bending Ash. A small, petite, African-American female, who was probably about 15.

Prior to coming into the program, Bending Ash had not ever been camping. She was a city girl through and through. Or at least had been prior to the program. She came from a fairly wealthy home, and was used to not breaking a sweat, or 'glistening,' as the females put it. Boys sweat; girls glisten.

Bending Ash was in staff camp, screaming, crying, but appearing to be intact. Her limbs were present and accounted for, there was no blood around her head and neck area, and she was upright. Surely, her voice was working, as evidenced by the shrill screams that challenged the silence of the still, peaceful and previously quiet night.

A female Instructor Abo went running over to Bending Ash. I, being the wise protector of our lives, maintained my vigilant defensive posture, with my eyes darting back and forth from side to side, looking for the danger that had chased Bending Ash into our camp. (Nothing, I might add, was to be found.)

After a few minutes, some gentle words, and reassuring hugs from the Instructor Abo to Bending Ash, she was finally able to calm down and tell us through her sobs that a giant 'cat' had passed through her camp.

Seriously! I thought. Wow. We had seen cougars in the area, but they usually did their best to avoid human contact and proximity.

This was a serious matter, and one that demanded that safety be the priority over the solo experience. So, after consulting with each other, the Instructor Abos set about to gather all of the students back in from solo.

Some of the testostrone-overwhelmed boys wanted to stay out on solo, and were simply hoping that a cat would venture into their camp. But we decided that everyone must come into the camp that night. There is safety in numbers.

After an hour long trek through the dark of the night, using our flashlights, stumbling, and finding some 'lost' Young Abos, we were able to get everyone near our fire, and settled down. Girls on one side, boys on the other. Staff in between. Same as every other night. And my peaceful night, that I just knew was going to be filled with great dreams, was just a memory.

The next morning, first thing, another Instructor Abo and I went to Bending Ash's camp to look at the tracks.

But, try as we might, we couldn't find any tracks.

The night before we had gone with flashlights, to collect her belongings, and whilst in the camp, looked for tracks. Not seeing any, we chalked it up to the darkness. However, even in the daylight, we couldn't find any tracks.

After looking all around Bending Ash's camp, and in fact, each of the camps, we determined that this was all a concocted story. When we went back to camp, rather than confronting Bending Ash directly with this information, we mentioned to the students that we would talk about this experience later that evening, after we had hiked the seven miles to our new camp.

Throughout the day, there was chatter amongst the group about what had happened. We gently released the information that there were no tracks found, and so, at the end our hiking that day, which was actually before lunch, it was understood by everyone that there was no danger from mountain lions.

When we did actually gather around the fire, and began our official discussion of the events of the night before, the group confronted Bending Ash. After very little push-back, she confessed to lying about the whole event. This time, her tears were real. A good discussion was had about fears (of the dark, of upsetting the group, etc.). A new solo date was planned, a few days from then, and when that solo took place, Bending Ash started again with her antics. But because her screams were so shrill and loud, most everyone else heard her, and in very little time, she was quieted by the rest of the students.

The rest of the solo experience was, for the most part, uneventful.

SWOLLEN GONAD

This day had been easy. We were hiking on the road. No vehicles had passed us during the entire four hours that we'd been hiking. It was still before noon, and we'd made good time.

Today we were going about twelve miles total, and being on the road had made this not only do-able, but also enjoyable.

We also had a few 'funnies' along the way. Today we'd introduced a new Instructor Abo to the Buffalo Berry bush.

Because Young Abos couldn't play tricks on Instructor Abos like this without appearing insubordinate, I took the lead. A few of the Young Abos had helped out, though.

We stopped along the road to take a break, and, what would you know - a Buffalo Berry bush!

Of course, we were all thirsty. So was this new Instructor Abo. He was a tough guy, though, and said he was doing fine.

But when the rest of us had taken drinks, he decided to break down and do the same.

Then, I casually mentioned the thirst-quenching qualities of the Buffalo Berry bush.

A few of the more tricky Young Abos had plucked some leaves from the bush and 'put them in their mouths,' to suck on them, as they were real thirst-quenchers!

But what they had really done was to drop the leaves on the ground, before ever reaching their mouths. It was convincing, nevertheless, and so Long Granite, the new Instructor Abo, decided to try the leaves, even if only for the experience.

When he was told to only take one, of course, he took a handful of leaves. His personality was the kind who would go over and above, just to prove that he could handle things.

Of course, we were all smiling. Smiling so much that I was afraid that he would catch on to the joke.

But, being too wrapped up in himself, he was oblivious to all of this, and filled his mouth with leaves.

We laughed.

All of us, that is, except Bending Willow.

Throughout the day, Bending Willow had lagged behind the rest of the group. I was often in front, but had heard the Instructor Abo member taking up the rear prodding Bending Willow along most of the time.

Odd, I thought, that Bending Willow would be so behind when he was one of the youth in fairly good shape, and would often be a leader, in fact.

Thinking back, the signs were clear. I just missed them because of my expectations of him.

Well, as we all laughed, I noticed that Bending Willow was grimacing. He was on the side of the road, sitting on the bank, and bent over forward. As the group conversation was focused on the new Instructor Abo, and his sudden need for more water, I made my way towards Bending Willow.

"What's up?" I asked him.

"Dave, I'm not feeling so well. I'm not feeling good at all, and I think I'm going to puke" he said.

This was actually the second day that Bending Willow said that he wasn't feeling well, but today it was worse.

And he really did look the part - eyes sunk in; furrowed brow; groans and moans.

I considered, as I looked at Bending Willow that late morning, that he may have something more wrong with him than just a flu.

When youth complained of an illness, the initial thought was always that they were faking it. The hikers would call each other on the 'fake' all the time.

But, looking at Bending Willow, I thought that he had a legit look of pain about him.

One of his buddies, who sort of hung out with Bending Willow, looked up and me and expressed the same thing.

"I think he's telling the truth, Dave. I think something's wrong."

I turned to look at Bending Willow, who was at this point looking at me.

"Dave, my ball is big. I mean, really big. And it hurts. It hurts bad."

Oh boy, I thought. What do I do with this?

Back in the late 80's, sexual abuse was a thing, but not a big thing.

"Counselor in Wilderness Program Looking at Boys Naked."

"Youth in Counseling Claims Counselor Touched Him."

I could see these headlines in the paper.

Or, I could see him making other allegations against me. I wasn't sure what, but I didn't want to find out.

Plus, add this to the fact that I just plain wasn't interested, and in fact, very repulsed, by doing what it would take to know if Bending Willow was telling the truth! I just plain didn't want to look that direction!

But, the pained look on his face compelled me to take seriously his complaint. He really did look to be in pain, and he really was acting much different than I had seen him act before.

So, I looked at Bending Willow and asked him what he wanted to do. He didn't know, and I wasn't sure.

It was about time to start hiking again, so we got everyone up and headed down the road. Bending Willow, with great effort, also stood up, but as he walked, he walked crouched down. Crouched down, and at about half the speed of everyone else.

Bending Willow looked at me, as I'd taken up the caboose position on our hike, and said that he just couldn't go on any more.

Wow - something must really be wrong.

His buddy was also hiking next to him, and looked at me with pleading eyes.

So, I made a decison that was way above my pay grade. I let the group continue to hike, but got the attention of the new counselor, Long Granite, and waved him back.

I told Bending Willow that we were going to go off the road a little ways; that we needed to make sure that he was telling the truth. Bending Willow was more than willing to do this. He also asked if his buddy, and fellow Youth Abo, could go with him. I looked at Long Granite, then said that his buddy could also come.

So, just in case someone did come by on the road, that had been vehicle-less for the past four hours, we went about 30 yards off the road, and out of sight from the road, Bending Willow pulled his pants down. As soon as he had done that, there was no doubt that he was telling the truth. The swollen testicle was indeed swollen. No more proof was needed in my mind.

I told him that we'd seen everything that we needed to see, and that he wasn't going to hike any more. Poor kid!

I couldn't imagine hiking the past two days, like he had. And I surely couldn't imagine him going on.

We went back to the road, and then I tried to figure out just what to do. Usually with a group of 9-12 students, there was a staff of three. One or two females, and one or two males, but usually only three.

That meant that either one Instructor Abo could go with Bending Willow, wherever he went, and two stay with the group, or vice versa. I knew that I couldn't just leave things the way they were.

I talked with the other Instructor Abo then, and we jointly decided that I ought to, somehow, get with Bending Willow to Teepee camp, where our section leader was. From there, Bending Willow could get the medical attention he needed. The other two Instructor Abo would remain with the group. They would hike just a mile or two more, go off to the side of the road about a quarter of a mile or so, and make camp.

With that decision made, the next question was - how would we get to Teepee camp?

Within minutes, where we had not seen a vehicle on the road, we saw dust. Heading the same way we needed to go was a local rancher. Stepping into the middle of the road, I flagged him down. And I suppose that flagging him down may give the wrong impression. Standing in the middle of the road, I basically forced him to stop.

Feeling a bit anxious about this whole situation, I walked over to his window, which he had rolled down, and explained to him that we had an urgent medical need, and wondered if he would be in a position to take us to our camp? Without hesitation, he graciously offered to do so.

After some brief, last-moment instructions, I got into the truck with Bending Willow. Off we went, to Teepee camp.

Like most ranchers, this fellow wasn't too talkative. If it's not needing to be said, it's not worth saying.

I don't know if he was in favor of the wilderness therapy program, or concept, or not. But I do know that he was happy to give us a ride.

As we bumped along the road, in silence, I notice Bending Willow wincing with each pothole we hit. And so, for the next ten miles, I sat next to the passenger door, grateful that we didn't have to hike to Teepee camp, and Bending Willow sat, wishing that the pain would go away.

Teepee camp was in a hidden box valley. Hidden at the bottom of a wooded valley, between two mountain ridges, with only one road leading in and out, it was an ideal spot to be concealed. But the rancher knew where to go and how to get there. I suspect that he was third or fourth generation in the area, and felt a keen sense that this was his country.

Well, as he drove into the area, which was only visited by people in the program. The couple who were the teepee 'residents,' and our section leader, Walking Agate, came out to meet us. The greetings were reserved, but kind.

When Walking Agate saw me sitting in the truck, and Bending Willow, his plain-faced look changed to a scowl. I could see, and sense, that he wasn't happy.

I didn't know what to expect from him. But I rather expected that, after he heard my story, he would be empathetic towards Bending Willow and give a me pat on the back for not only doing the right thing, but getting a ride into camp.

Neither of these things happened.

After thanking the rancher, he pulled away and left.

I turned towards Walking Agate, and he proceeded to lay into me about having someone bring us to camp, about leaving the group, and simply disrupting his day.

Still, being patient, I proceeded to explain to him that Bending Willow had a problem, and that it was a serious one.

He didn't hear me. And continued to lay into me.

This type of behavior took it's toll on my patience, and I began to bite back. Not hard, but even the little nipping got his attention. He stopped yelling, and it was my turn.

I told him about the hard time that Bending Willow was having hiking, about his enlarged testicle, which was about the size of a grapefruit, and about the ride to Teepee camp.

I then said that this problem was no longer mine, but was his to deal with. But I firmly suggested that he not ignore the problem, because it had already gone on for days. And any permanent damage could be made worse if he didn't act on it.

He calmed down, and went to talk with the Teepee camp couple. A few minutes later he came back, asked Bending Willow to go with him, and he and the fellow running Teepee camp took Bending Willow into the Teepee and looked for themselves.

Within minutes Walking Agate was on his way to town, and to the clinic.

I stayed with the couple at Teepee camp and helped them to make ready to fire some clay bowls and mugs that they were teaching us to make.

A number of hours later Walking Agate came back into camp, with Bending Willow. There was an infection, and though not life-threatening, or even permanently damaging, it was nonetheless severe, and it was a good thing that Bending Willow had gone in. He was given some medication to take for the next week.

Because it was so late, Bending Willow and I stayed at Teepee camp that night.

The couple slept in the Teepee. Walking Agate slept in his camp, which was more of a semi-permanent dwelling. Bending Willow and I slept outside, under the stars, near the Teepee.

When it was quiet, and the only sound was the night life talking with each other, and the breeze going through the trees, Bending Willow spoke.

"Dave."

"Ya," I said.

"Thanks for believing me. And thanks for sticking up for me. Thanks for helping."

"You're welcome, Bending Willow. Sleep well."

WATER, WATER, WHO WANTS SOME WATER

"When the well's dry, we know the worth of water."

Benjamin Franklin

"Tank up."

Every time we were near water, this was the clarion call.

Hiking, outdoors, in the desert, water was the life-blood. We take air for granted, but water, well, not so. Water was scarce.

So, we would all gather around the water, be it a spring, a watering trough, or a 55 gallon drum, and fill our water bottles, move to the side, drink as much as we could, then get back in line for more.

This we would do until we were 'waterlogged,' and then, we would do another half a canteen.

Those who were new to this way of outdoor life would drink until they couldn't hold their breath anymore, then stop. Their drinking was gauged by their lung capacity. This was on day one.

On day two, they would know what 'tank up' really meant. Now, their drinking was gauged by the fulness of their tummy.

In civilization, most of us don't give a second thought about water and where it comes from. A tap, of course! Just like milk comes from the supermarket. Right?! In the desert, every drop was precious.

In the wilderness survival circles, there is a common reference principle known as the *Rules of Three*. This is so well known that there seems to be no debate about it. A person can live only three minutes without air, three days without water, three weeks without food, and three months without some sort of human contact.

When we think of 'surviving,' it's usually the food stuff that we think about. That's because our tummy is so loud when it's empty that it tends to drown out all of the other cries for attention.

But really, it's water that we need, that is much more important, than is food. We need water. Our body needs water. Our mind needs water. To digest food, we need water.

Water breeds life.

Wind

Wind, oh, the wind!

There *were* times that the wind was pleasant, or rather, the breeze was pleasant. When a three-mile-per-hour zephyr kissed us, it left us with a touch of coolness. How nice this felt. Just like the soft touch of a lover's hand, it brought a sense of peace.

But, this occurred only, or nearly only, in the mid-morning hours. And it was a welcomed relief. During the afternoon and early evening hours, the wind-machine seemed to be turned up to high. Fifteen or twenty mile per hour winds were not uncommon. In July and August, this was often accompanied by rain. This was the rainy season.

I think of what Edward Abbey wrote in his book *Desert Solitaire*. The amount of water in the desert is just the right amount.

The complaints of humans come when we introduced into the desert that which is not naturally there, namely, us.

Well, it's not a normal or a natural thing, for either the people or the desert, to have a group of 8-12 kids, and 3 or 4 staff, tromping over the sand, the cryptograph, around head-high sage brush, and through juniper and pinion pine forests, on a day that any normal-thinking person would be out of the 100 degree weather, when 20 MPH winds were blowing.

But then again, it's not a normal thing for the kids to behave the way they did at home. Nor was it normal for the kids to be so far removed from nature that they spent a fair portion of their time adjusting to fresh air, sunlight, hiking, drinking plain water, and 'toughening up.' I guess, as I think about it, this was a summer of all sorts of 'not-normal'!

SHEEP KILL

As I entered the camp, Blue Juniper came up to me smiling the biggest smile I've ever seen, and was holding something in front of her that looked hauntingly like a stuffed balloon. A grey, 'earthy' stuffed balloon. Her blond hair was done up something like Wilma Flintstone's red hair - it was in a rough sort of bun, with a stick holding it in place. However, Wilma was actually a lot more clean than Blue Juniper, who hadn't seen a shower or bath in weeks.

"Look! Look what we've got!" she said excitedly.

I looked, and all I saw was something that looked like a brownish rubber bag of some sort that was about 5 inches in diameter, hanging down due to the weight of something inside of it. I cocked my head, squinted a bit, twisted my mouth a bit, because that always helps a person think, you know, and looked harder.

"Hmmm," I said. "Well, I must say, I'm stumped."

I looked back at Blue Juniper, and her smiling face melted into a flat look. The bouncy, bubbly person who ran up to greet me was visibly disappointed that I had no idea what it was that she was holding.

I had just returned from my day off, which was actually a bit over a day this time, and I had come into camp in the early evening hours. There were three of the groups together. We rarely all got together, but this was a special time. It was the *Sheep Kill*.

I'm sure that there's a more appropriate term for it; a term that isn't so 'in the face,' but *Sheep Kill* is what we called it. Towards the end of our three weeks together, two sheep were brought into the camp, and they were 'dispatched,' and used for food, tools, etc.

It is actually a very good lesson in life. Growing up in Montana, and working on ranches, and living for a while on a ranch where sheep were raised, I came to appreciate the usefulness of animals, the sacredness of life, the fragility of life, and our stewardship of morality when a life was taken. The *Sheep Kill* provided this to the participants.

Most of the children were from the city, and if they had seen sheep, it was through a car window, on a field trip, or in books. But here, when two sheep were brought into camp for the express purpose of feeding the children, it was a real life lesson.

There were no Native American rituals involved in this experience, but some of the Native principles were taught to the children at this time. We thanked our Creator for providing the sheep. We thanked the sheep for providing their lives. We thanked those who went before us, who brought forth knowledge of how to use the various parts of the sheep. We thanked each other, for sharing this experience with us.

Blue Juniper was holding the intestines of the sheep. The children had already killed the sheep, and were in the process of using every part of the sheep.

"This," she said, "is sausage."

Realization came to my mind, and I smiled. And when I smiled, her excitement bounded back.

"I'm getting ready to boil it. You can have some when it's done."

"Thank you," I said. "That will be great."

She ran off, back to the camp, where her water was boiling, and put the 'sausage' into the pot to cook.

Another student, a male standing nearby, made his way towards me. We stood together, watching the scene, and then I asked him, "Winding Branch, just what is it that's in the sausage?"

He looked over at me, smiled, and said, "Are you sure you wanna know?"

The way he said it, and the twinkle in his eye, convinced me that I DID want to know. And I wanted to know if he was going to eat it too?!

"Yup. Tell me." I said.

"Well, anything that can't be roasted or grilled is in the sausage," he said. "The kidneys, the brain, and some of the smaller muscles."

Having just come back from my day off, I was full. My belly was filled to the brim with good, old, fake fast food. And hearing the description of what the youth were cooking, I found myself thinking that my biggest problem was going to be declining the delicasies without offending any of them. Not having had meat for weeks, they were protein-ready, and even with sheep, which most of them had never tasted, they were willing participants in the feast.

And feast it was! The camp was buzzing with people cutting, cooking, creating, gorging. Usually we headed to bed about 9ish or a bit after. This night, however, nobody went to sleep until about 2 in the morning.

Earlier in the day, when I was gone, this is what happened.

The three different groups, by design, converged on the same location within a few hours of each other. Most of the children didn't know each other, but most of the staff did. But they began mingling, and within minutes had made good relationships. That's what hard circumstances to do people. They bring folks together.

About 3 PM, there were two sheep that were brought into the camp. As a precursor to this, the group was called together, all at once, and instructed about what was going to happen.

The sacredness of life was discussed. The seriousness of taking life from anything, including animals was emphasized. And the importance of not wasting any part of the animal was discussed. There were some staff members who had been involved with previous sheep kills, and they took the lead in teaching the group about what was going to happen.

Every part of the sheep was going to be used. The hides would be tanned and made into mittens. The insides would be cut into small pieces and stuffed into the cleaned-out intestines, to be made into sausage. The meat would be roasted over the fire and consumed. The sinew would used to fasten leather. The bones would be used for tools and decoration. Even the blood was going to be collected, and used in the preparation of the sausage.

I wasn't there, but I heard that two of the youth were chosen to be the ones to slit the throats of the sheep. And neither of them ended up doing it. People talk tough, but when it comes right down to it, tough talk doesn't mean tough people. Well, of course, that depends of how you define tough. But in this case, tough didn't mean that the life of a sheep could be taken by slitting the throat. Two boys were chosen, and though they were the rough sort of kids who one would think would NOT have a problem with the task, neither of them ended up killing the sheep. As it turned out, one of the sheep was killed by a young lady who was somewhat quiet, but who had changed quite a bit over the few short weeks that she'd been out there. The other was killed by a boy who was, by all accounts, shy and rather timid.

This was one of the toughest parts of the whole process.

The meat was welcomed, the rest was welcomed, the socializing was welcomed, but the killing - most people never see the beginning of the process of where their food comes from.

And so it was that the children were taught how sacred life is, and that day it became a very real thing to sincerely appreciate the hamburger in front of them or the pepperoni on their pizza.

SKINNY RUNNERS AND OTHER STORIES

Skinny Runners

They usually come out at dusk, and run into the night. Walking is possible, but very foreign to them.

Thus it was that he came into our camp, and all of us unaware of it. He came into our camp to take a pot. Because, they still need to eat. But rather than making their own containers in which to cook, they found it much easier to take ours. Metal. Much more durable and functional. And pretty. Gotta remember the pretty!

What is he? What are they?

Skinny Runners.

Skinny runners are the things of legend. They haven't ever been seen and conversed with. It's just understood that they exist.

Because nobody has ever really seen one, and I mean, really seen one, most people classify them in the category of Bigfoot. There are signs that point to their existence, but nobody has yet to take a photograph of one.

Each night around the campfire, we would tell stories. One of the stories that came up time and again involved skinny runners.

Skinny runners are the ancestors of the Ancient Ones, the Anasazi. They have inhabited the land for centuries, and probably even Millenia, and are the keepers of the secrets of the land. They are also protectors. Protectors of the land, the graves, the holy sites, *and* the people who go into the deserts today.

Skinny runners are so skinny, that when they turn sideways, they can't be seen. Even directly in front of you, if standing sideways, they are invisible. Playing cards have nothing over skinny runners, being 10X fatter than these slender folks.

I don't remember ever talking about gender. They're always male in the stories, though there must be females as well.

And protectors? Well, at least most of them are protectors. Some have turned to the 'dark side,' and as such, cause problems and stir up trouble. But these kind are fewer than the good kind. And the good ones will not hurt the 'bad ones,' but they will stop their shenanigans, if they can.

And they joke. They play around. They move things. Put your knife down, turn around to look at something, then turn right back. Your knife is moved. Or it's missing. Who knows why. But we know how.

The Skinny Runners.

Skinny Runners are a part of the desert folklore. At night, around the fires, after dinner, to avoid talk of food, stories would be told. And stories would be added upon, and the legends would grow.

We would often take turns starting a story, then passing it along to the next person in the circle. They would add a thought or two, develop a plot, or change the plot, then pass it on. And soon, Skinny Runners began to take on a life of their own.

Chameleon in nature, they can not only turn sideways and become invisible to the human eye, but they can also change their skin color to blend in with their surroundings. Movement is the only give-away in these situations. And they are great at standing still, for minutes on end.

Most people have seen a movement out of the corner of their eye, and not known it was a skinny runner, but it was. And some have seen what looked like a shadow move, only to blink and not see it again. In the desert - these are skinny runners!

Creation and Imagination

As I have mentioned elsewhere, there were evenings, sitting around the fire, that a staff member, and sometimes a youth participant, would start a story, then pass it along. Each person would take a turn adding a few sentences to the story. Sometimes each person in the group, or circle, would have five or six turns to add to the story.

There was good fun, as well as good problem-solving, involved in this.

One could think ahead, about what he wanted to add, but really, with ten people adding to the story, by the time it came around to you again, the story line could be totally different than at your last turn. And so what you wanted to say would often no longer fit. So, we all had to think on our feet, so to speak. And we had to listen well to the others, and make what we said fit in, to some large degree, with what was being said.

PRE-EPILOGUE

It's been nearly 30 years since my experience in the wilderness. Or at least, the experience that I've related throughout this book. The desert still calls to me, and sometimes I heed the call.

It's hard to live in this society after having been touched by that way of life. It's like the song by the Bellamy Brothers:

He's an old hippie

And he don't know what to do

Should he hang on to the old

Should he grab on to the new

He's an old hippie

This new life is just a bust

He ain't tryin to change nobody

He's just tryin real hard to adjust

Recently I've read (listened to) the book by Edward Abbey, *Desert Solitaire*. That was a thoroughly fascinating time I spent with Ed, relating to some of the experiences he recounted, whilst totally not relating to other experiences. He commands the language in a beautiful, magnificent, moving manner.

I remember during that summer of 1989, having his book recommended to me. But, I didn't give it a second thought. And frankly, I think that I would have been wholly turned off by it back then.

But age brings slowness, and contemplation, and a desire for quality and not quantity. This is where I find myself now, and so I've taken the time to explore avenues that I haven't taken the time to explore earlier in life. This book was one of those avenues. I can say that I would recommend the book. Fifty years old, and it has created a cult following.

I would also say that I'm excited to get the book *Desert Cabal* by one Amy Irvine. From what I can tell, this is a 'rebuttal book' to *Desert Solitaire*, and is written as *an alternate version* of Abbey's book. Or maybe not so much an alternate version, but a sound verbal spanking of Abbey and his steeped-in-culture social mores from which he viewed the world. I think that it will be the literature form of a cat-fight, and I like things like this, as it get's people to think. It gets me to think.

However, I digress a bit. Because both of these books, though addressing certain aspects of the wilderness, and the desert in particular, also have the politics and morals of the management of the outdoors as a primary focus. On the other hand, my experience in the wilderness that I attempted to convey here is about the understanding of our human psyche, and relationships, as found in nature.

The desert is a healing place. It is a natural for wilderness therapy programs to be located in the desert. And, as long as human beings don't get in the way, the desert can effect amazing change on a person.

The desert is both predictable and unpredictable. This is one of those things that make her such a healing place. We learn to do what we can, and when we can't *do,* we have *done* to us. We 'experience.' We don't control. We don't force or manipulate.

There have been wilderness survival programs come and go. The program that I worked with had many good people working for it, and many great people enrolled as youth participants. But the structure of the program made it seem that humans were doing the work of changing in the desert. Truly, the change was being done in the desert on humans, by nature.

Those programs that adopt the philosophy of safety first, then a gentle, loving guidance by humans whilst Mother Nature does her job, are those programs that succeed.

I think back 29 years ago, and wonder what my former 'students' are doing now. They would be 41 to 46 years old today. Maybe even some of them grandparents! What would they write? What was good for them? What was not good? Were the 2 or 3 months they spent in the wilderness as impactful on them as it was on me? Do they know that I wonder how they're doing, and how genuinely concerned about them I was then? And am today?

In this day and age when our knowledge grows nearly exponentially daily, but our wisdom diminishes at about the same rate, we need something to change. In our fight for freedom, we don't even know what to do with it once we get it. It's time we figure out what freedom really is, and how to use this freedom.

EXHILARATIONS

The Beginning & the Ending

The sunrise and sunset. Those! Those are highlights.

In an urban area, the sun is often far into the sky before we actually take notice of the light. And then it seems that we curse it rather than bless it. But in the desert, the sun brings with it many things: warmth; life; light; sight.

The sounds of the desert are many at night. But about 30 minutes before sunrise, the environment becomes more still. The night animals find their holes for the day. The night insects spirit themselves into the shadows and shade of the plants and the earth. And the day-life is not yet alive; not yet moving. This time is a sacred time. It is an anticipatory time, and a time of grief both. But more anticipatory. The loss of the stillness of the night is grieved. The rest that will soon be put to bed, the rest that occurs at night, the loss of this rest, that is grieved.

But also anticipated is the freedom that light brings with it. Freedom to move around with less fear of being injured by lack of sight. Freedom to be an active participant in the movement that creates good things. Freedom to contribute, rather than just sit back and enjoy and appreciate. Light brings life, activity, and production.

Desert Varnish

When God paints in the desert, he uses the rain. The rain and minerals.

The rain, hitting the rocks and the sand, paints an auditory picture of clean, of pure, of new, of renewal.

And look at the desert right after a rain, when the sun comes out. See the new-ness of life. The flowers that open, saying thank you for the moisture. The skittering of bugs across the wet sand. The playing amonst the small puddles left in the rocks. The fleeting rainbow.

But really, what is so impressive to me are the paintings that come from the rain.

Desert Varnish is God's way of leaving His mark on the desert, bold, for all to see.

The oranges, blacks and browns that streak the rocks a hundred feet high or more, are left after centuries of rains move the minerals in the earth from their deposits, sometimes buried deep within the earth, onto the face of the rocks.

Even the greatest of all artists cannot create works that compare with this natural painting. To feel truly like nothing, and yet like you are everything, stand a hundred yards away and look at the Desert Varnish paintings happening before your eyes. See the canvas, then see the watercolors happen before your eyes, then see the sun come out and illuminate the slightly-altered painting. What joy!

Minimalist

I love that everything that I need to survive is on my back. And actually, this isn't true. Everything I need to survive is on my back and in my head.

Cody Lundin, a premier survival instructor today, has stated that 'The More You Know, the Less You Need." And it's true.

If one knows and looks, the desert is filled with life, with food, and even water can be found. It is, all of it, hidden from the casual observer, but in truth, there is abundance.

And what a great feeling that one can go for a week into the desert, the seemingly inhospitable environment, and not only survive, but also thrive.

Top of the World

The Carpenter's of 1960's fame, sang a song about being on top of the world, looking down on creation. It's a fun song. My dad listened to it, and so I listened to it.

As I stood on the tops of the ridges, that only fit people could get to, and where I would be surprised if another human being in the last 200 years walked, I would find myself humming this song.

Looking down from heights that nearly touched the clouds was exhilarating.

Granted - it wasn't Mt. Everest.

But, it was the Everest of the Kapairowits plateau.

Sagebrush

It's said that the sagebrush is the only home and environment that the Sage Grouse can survive in. And that the sage is disappearing from the western landscape.

It could be that the Sage grouse is also disappearing, because in all of my hiking through sage, I never did scare any grouse out. There were (hungry) times I would have liked to scare a grouse or two out. But alas, no such luck.

The sagebrush, however, provided other benefits for me. The shade under a 7' sage was welcomed in the warm afternoon sun. It was a great thing to have shade, and when the only plant for a mile was a sage brush, then having it be 7' tall, and leafed out, was welcomed.

The smell of sage, and especially after a rain, is one that I still cherish to this day.

And bow drills - the sage was used for bow drill sets. Personally, I found yucca and cottonwood to my liking much more than sage. But some of the students used sage, and used it successfully, in making fire.

Gratitude

Being thanked never got old. You will recall the story of the swollen gonad, and how I was thanked for believing Bruce. That felt good. To be recognized, on a human level, for being a positive part of someone's life.

In the moment, there were times that I was thanked. When a student busted his first coal with the bow drill with my assistance; when I gave some of my weekly food ration to a student who had run out. I was thanked at these times, but it felt like a 'forced' thanks. You know the difference.

But the unprovoked 'thanks,' the times that someone volunteered verbal gratitude simply because they were feeling gratitude, those were the meaningful times. In the program, and in life, these are the 'thanks' that provide an exhilaration to me (and you).

Finding Water

I've never been so (something) as when we found wet sand, and then seeping water, at the bottom of the hole we dug in the unnamed wash in the middle of nowhere. Happy doesn't cut it. Grateful comes closer. But it's even more than this. It's knowing that life really will go on.

I think back to this experience in the program, that I wrote about in an earlier chapter, of having to dig for water, and then finding it. And I compare my mood to what I see in plants that are wilted from lack of water. That's something observable.

The water-deficient plant will droop. It will close up, and begin to slouch. It can't fill the measure of it's creation, whatever that measure is. Beauty is hidden, and vanishes. Serving as sustenance for animals is minimized, and eventually disappears. Without water, the plant becomes a blight on the land, rather than adding to the beauty.

But picture this: a dehydrated flower, petals closed, drooping, dying. Then - thunderclouds, wind (to wake the flower up), coolness, rain. Moisture! And, minutes later, the flower revived, is standing tall, beauty restored. A beauty that was there all along, but just in hiding.

This is what the water did to me and the two others who searched for water. It showed outwardly, by our smiles, our spunky conversation, our renewed sense of energy. And it showed inwardly - the zippy attitude, the 'we can do this' determination, and the renewed excitement to meet the night and the day.

Finding water was an exhilaration.

Bustin' a Coal

Honestly, I don't remember the first time that I busted a coal. Probably because, over the course of that Summer and the year following, I made thousands of fires from the bow-drill. Multiple times each day I would help students 'bust a coal.' I would show them, then we would do a double bow-drill (yes, I also count these times).

But really, it's simply amazing to me to see fire come from rubbing wood together. And to think that, within the components of the bow-drill set, a fire is there already. We just need to put everything together in the right way. In the right order, after creating the right set of circumstances, we can be a participant in eliciting fire from natural components! It's simply mind-boggling to me.

This never got old to me. Bustin' a coal.

Even today I watch people make a bow-drill fire, and I stand in awe, watching this amazing process. It's still magical to me. It's art in action, and is a real joy to see.

Thunderstorms

Only a few times was I privileged to be in a natural shelter, a cave or overhang, whilst the heavens roared and thundered! And not only the thunder, that sometimes deep sound of rumble, and sometimes the ear-splitting sound of shrieking, but also the lightening. I've seen some spectacular Independence Day fireworks shows, and some really cool laser shows in a Planetarium, but NOTHING compares to the spectacular show put on by the Gods during this renewal of all renewals in the desert.

Someone once wrote, "The more brutal the storm the calmer my heart." This is me!

Rather than run to a corner and shrink, I find my safe place and enjoy the amazing grandeur of the power of nature! Do I mind feeling so small, so powerless, so 'nothing?' Nope.

INTROSPECTIONS

Daily Journal Writing

"I ate a lizard today."

"Nighthawk got us up about two hours before sunrise, and we started hiking. I guess that's OK, though, because it was cool. We got to our camp, set up, ate lunch and worked on our bow drill fires and traps."

The youth, and the staff, were given a spiral bound notebook at the beginning of each section. One of the requirements, daily, was to keep a journal. This journal offered time for introspection; looking inside to see what could happen to create more happiness and contentment.

Of all the 'man-made requirements' that the Young Abos had to endure whilst on the program, the journal was the most helpful one, in my opinion. Writing in a journal was an opportunity that allowed one time to think, deep if desired, about life, and about what was wanted.

Most of the Young Abos, prior to their participation in the program, didn't take time to think about their life. They were, like so many of us in many ways, swept along in life, and rather than control our boat by the rudder, allow the winds that blow to take our boat where the wind blows. We don't realize that we really do have some control over direction.

Oh, we get this to some degree. What is our major in college going to be, or what job will we work at? Who will I marry? What kind of car do I want to buy? But that's piddly stuff. The really important stuff that matters, our psyche, is something that we can also control. Our mind. Our moods. And this was the beauty of the journal. This is a 'release' from prison, if we'll let it be. The key to realizing that we have responsibility, or put another way, the ability to respond!

I didn't know this then, but have since discovered that a study was commissioned by some counselors, psychotherapist, wherein the question was asked, is there anything that works as good as counseling, in helping folks overcome depression and anxiety? Of course, the counselors wanted to show that there was nothing that works as good as counseling for depression and anxiety. If this could be shown, the existence of their (our) profession could be justified.

Well, as it turns out, the study did show that there are TWO things that work as well as counseling in treating depression and anxiety. These two things are .... (holding your breathe?):

Gardening

Journal Writing

Folks who participated in these two activities experienced a positive change in the same degree as if they went to counseling!

Cool, huh!

And free. Which makes it even more cool.

Now, don't ask me to point to the source of this study. I read this about two decades ago, and I don't think that even Google could find the source. Because, I rather think that counselors would have squashed the study by now, and gone back to the territorial position that nothing helps as good as counseling.

But hey, I'm a believer. Just talk with any gardener, and you'll find little depression. Or at least depression that is managed and made less by gardening. What is it about gardening? Playing in the dirt? Sunlight? Facilitating growth in plants? Who knows. But it works.

Same with journal writing. After the initial phase of 'I don't know what to write," or "I sound so dumb when I read what I wrote,' the journal-writers realize that they think through their problems and their solutions, and putting it on paper really does help.

Thus it is that I believe that the Journal took the place of counselors in the program. And most likely did just as well.

Not that counselors are of benefit. It would have been ideal to have both a journal as well as a counselor. Having someone to bounce ideas and thoughts off of is often invaluable. But the counseling must also be good. No counselor is better than a bad counselor.

So, every day Young Abos and Instructor Abos wrote in our journals. I've got mine, scanned now, and someday may post them, along with explanations. They really did bring insight to me that was otherwise locked up inside. Same with the students.

Value for Life

Hiking in the valleys of the Kapairowits Plateau, we would often have contact with some of the local yocals. I say this in all kindness. Really. There were some really descent, nice ranchers who would frequent the roads that we hiked on. We waved. Occasionally we would talk. And as I mentioned, one went miles out of his way at one time to get a student and me to Teepee Camp, for the medical crisis being experienced. Good folk. Really good folk.

Plus, we would often use their stock tanks for water. When our water drop was dry, or when we just stumbled upon a water tank, near a spring, we'd tank up. What a welcome relief in the water-sparse country.

Near a water tank was the one time that I saw a mountain lion whilst I was out there, FYI.

But there was one time that I really got upset.

We topped a small rise, in a rather high valley, near a road, and there before us were acres and acres of juniper trees and sagebrush that had been 'chained!'

The site of it made me nearly nauseous. And just thinking about it now, 30 years later, still tips my tummy upside down. The wanton disregard for the thousands of plants that had been needlessly killed, all for a few acres of grazing ground, I assume.

'Chaining' is when a super-strong chain is connected to two bulldozers, and the bulldozers go forward, side by side, pulling the chain between them. Anything in the way of the chain is uprooted. Usually this is sage, but it's also juniper trees. And Rabbit Brush. And Buffalo Berry. And Pinion Pine. Etc., etc. It takes big bulldozers, and a mighty chain, to do the wanton destruction that occurs.

Now, I'm no Sierra Club member, but .... I could be.

Same with the NRA. I could be a member.

I like to think that I see a situation outside of the political glasses that so many people want us to put on.

But seeing these trees and the brush torn up, and just left there (It would be removed, I'm sure. Probably piled up and burned. Rather, pushed into a pile by the same dozers that uprooted them, and then burned. Leaving all of the animals that depended on them for shelter, and food, homeless and hungry), leaves a hole in my heart. There was no irrigation in the area. So the grasses that would be planted, if any, would be dry grasses, which one could justifiably argue were no better than what was removed. All to make enough feed for an extra cow or two. Uugghhh.

Life. We were taught to respect life. Life would be provided to us, if we didn't fight with Mother Nature. Water. Food. Animals. Plants. Shelter. All of it provided for us, if we were just good stewards, and worked in conjunction with Mother Nature, rather than try to fight her.

And yet, we saw the wanton taking of life by chaining.

I did NOT sabotage the dozers, or the chains. I didn't even think of it. But looking back, I wonder why I didn't.

But even typing this now, I know why I didn't and why I wouldn't. It's not in my nature to do this, nor is it in my nature to set this sort of example for the Young Abos.

Cryptogram. The living soil. I've mentioned this before in this book. I was taught by Richard what Cryptographic soil was, and given a reverence for it, so that when ever we were in an area where there was a trail, we followed it.

Most wild game trails are usually in the best place they can be. Meaning, they choose the best way to get from Point A to Point B. This made it easy to follow the game trails, and to stay off the cryptogram.

The winds, usually in the afternoons, picked up quite a bit. A breeze was welcomed. The winds were not. We'd hunker down, behind our strung-out tarps, behind rocks, behind an earth berm, or an overturned tree, or against a cliff, when the winds kicked up.

The sand would, of course, be kicked up with the winds. Then it would blow. Into our hair, our eyes, our eyebrows, our ears and nose, into our clothes, our shoes, and our wool blankets. And it would blow into the bark on the junipers and the sage, and it would blow on down the valleys.

All of us, environmentally-minded or not, would have appreciated less sand in the air and more on the ground. So we were all in favor, for selfish reasons, to not step on the cryptogram soil, because this meant that there was this much less sand blowing around.

You see, when a footprint broke the cryptogram, the sand became a free agent, or rather, an un-free agent. It was no longer kept in place, but with even just ONE STEP, it was loosened up, and allowed to, with the next wind, move on down the line. Sometimes the end of that line came at our body, the next tree or bush, or possibly into a wash where, with the next rain, it would be deposited a mile away.

We cared about the cryptogram. The life that it was. And the life that it allowed around it. We were inconvenienced by the blowing sands. But burrowing animals were greatly impacted by such things as blowing sands. So were the sage grouse, the snakes, the scorpions, the ants, and all of life. This was their home. We were interlopers. Wannabe residents, but in the end, just interlopers.

MY WILDERNESS THERAPY

Crossing the Water

We stopped, *again*, at the edge of the river, the Escalante River, so that Aaron could take off his hiking boots, don his water shoes, and cross. He didn't want to get his hiking boots wet. But, after the sixth time in less than an hour, with about four minutes for each shoe swap, it was starting to get on the nerves of everyone. 'Everyone' included the seven staff hiking in to meet our groups of students, after completing our week of training. Actually, there were five new staff and two seasoned staff members.

I looked at our group. There was me. I took my shoes off at the first crossing, then when told that there would be many more crossings, I just followed the lead of the seasoned staff, and left my shoes on. The others did the same. Aaron - no such thing.

I wondered how long he would make it out here. How long would this fellow, who was used to a shower-a-day, be willing to live sleeping on the ground, eating on a log, and picking ash cakes up from the coals? I didn't have to wonder for more than a few days. Within a week, he was gone, headed into the un-wild blue civilized yonder.

After getting out of the vehicle, a Bronco that we had all crammed into, it was a relief to finally be hiking. The mid-afternoon sun wasn't yet hot this late May day, like it would be two months from then. As we left civilization, my first time leaving civilization in the desert, I was, frankly, a bit trepidatious. The longest that I had known any of the people I was with was a week.

But, as we settled into hiking the six miles to meet up with the groups of youth who were in the program, my nerves also started to settle. After ten minutes of hiking, the clear clean air filled my lungs, my legs were warmed up with the kinks worked out of them, and the tarp-and-blanket pack on my back had settled in to a comfortable position.

Paradox, Truth, Freedom

It was morning, and I rousted myself out of bed, at daylight. This was actually a late morning for me. Often, our group would get up about 4 AM, hike for a bit, and then stop for breakfast. But since we were staying in the same camp for a few nights, there was no reason to be up early to hike. Later in the day we would go on a four or five mile hike, just to get out and about, but our current camp was 'home.'

There were, on occasions, that I would allow myself the luxury of sleeping in. I say luxury, but truly, getting up early are what I remember most fondly of my times in the desert. There was no wind in the mornings (usually), it was quiet, the coyotes had settled down from their concert of the night before, and except for the occasional snoring or movement heard from the people in our group, all was still.

Oh, one could listen closely and hear movement. The scamper of a mouse across the sand and rock, the sprint of squirrel's feet moving from one branch to another in the moon light bathed environment. And an occasional creaking from the decades-old junipers that surrounded our camp, adjusting to yet another day in the high desert atmosphere, preparing to take in the relentless rays of the sun and resist the afternoon winds that served only to make the tree stand more firm.

And the stars. The canopy of stars, that made it seem as if there was indeed a roof over our heads, illuminated by thousands of flickering candles. Many a night I recall laying in my tarp and wool blanket, looking up into the night sky, wondering about my teeny tiny little place in the universe. Feeling so small, so insignificant, so powerless, and yet at the same time, being filled with something that is truly indescribable. This 'something' gave me reason to continue on, and to even be empowered by the fact that although I was less than a blip on the eternal radar, there was a part of what I was a part of that was significant in the grand scheme of it all.

Paradox. I thought often of paradox. 'He that is greatest among you shall be the servant of all.' The greatest is the least? So to strive to be known, one must purposely try to be unknown?

Truth is the way to enlightenment, and enlightenment brings peace, and yet truth is often hard to hear. What is peaceful about that?

And freedom. The youth I was working with desired freedom. Craved freedom. Many of them, if not all, would choose behaviors in their effort to assert their freedom, only to have these behaviors bind them, and take away their freedom. 'Don't smoke,' they were told. And so, to assert their freedom, they would start smoking, and thus become addicted. Freedom from parents, and societal expectations, but finding themselves being bound by more significant chains.

The hours of contemplation and conversation I had with the starry heavens were a peaceful time. But one of thought, with some answers, but mostly more questions.

It is said that darkness is indicative of evil, of Satan, of wickedness. And yet, I found that my most peaceful moments occurred at night, I'm guessing about 2 AM, when I would be awakened by some night sound, and not be able to go back to sleep. Why did I find such solace in the stillness of the night, when the stars and moon were the night lights?

Was I evil? Did I feel most at home in the darkness? Was I kidding myself, in all of my goals? Did I really know the difference between good and evil? What, really, was I really like, deep down? My true nature?

Dreams & Resilience

And as I lay, contemplating on these deeper thoughts, I also wondered on some of the more simple thoughts that are common to most people - Who would I marry? What about children? What would life be like in my family?

Oh, I had it all planned out. We would be like the Sackett's, in the frontier novels written by Louis L'Amour. When one family member was in trouble, we would all come a-runnin'. Troubles were meant to be faced together, and this is how it would be in my family. Forget the fact that I hadn't yet seen a family really operate this way. MY family would be different!

(Twenty-nine years later, I smile as I think back to this time. Being naive is a vital part of youth. Without the unrealistic dreams of how life is supposed to be and will be, we wouldn't have hope. And hope is exactly the thing that carries us through the otherwise hopeless times of life.)

How has my family turned out? Just exactly the way I trained them to be! NOT the way I envisioned, but the way I trained them to be.

Thank God for resilience. For them. For me.

Thank God that we are NOT only a product of our environment. For them. For me.)

Remembering back to my life in the desert, I realize that it had become a home for me that was as comfortable as any home I'd ever been in. And in some ways, it was better. Everything I needed to survive I carried on my back and in my head. Cody Lundin, one of the most wise of survivalists and preppers, says that the more you know, the less you need. So true! There are YouTube sites, books, blogs, and conventions about minimizing, or becoming minimalists. This was my life, that 1989 Summer. And it was a good life. A great life.

Nine Square Feet

One of the exercises that we would have the youth do was to have them spread out. No telling why, and with no other direction than this, they distanced themselves.

After everyone had found a spot, usually within 10 or 15 years of another person, we would give these instructions: mark out a square in front of you, three feet by three feet. They would do this.

Now, for the next hour you will observe what is happening in this bit of real estate in front of you. Record your findings in your journal. Record everything. EVERYTHING. No talking; just see, and write.

The lists were all alike, as you can probably imagine.

Within a minute, (and sometimes up to three minutes for the really observant ones), the 'stuff' that was within this nine square feet was written on the paper.

Sand. Dirt. Sticks. Leaves. Juniper berries. Juniper tree. Ants. Unidentified bugs. All of this was identified as what was in the 'box.'

Even though the instructions were to not talk, inevitably one of the youth would say, "I'm done. I can't find any more." To which I would respond, "No talking. Keep looking. We're here for an hour."

A collective sigh would be heard, but, what else could they do? Mutiny?! No. So, back to the box everyone would go.

Now, here's where individuality kicked in.

Some of the youth would look more deeply, and find some other 'things' that were not as readily observed at first glance: an ant trail; a scorpion covered mostly by sand; a small plant, trying to eek out an existence, found to be just barely poking through the ground. There was more, under the surface.

For some, this is as far as the observation went. Their hour was spent at this level. And it brought boredom.

But for others, they became fascinated by what was really happening. In all of life, I've come to believe that there are at least three levels of 'meaning,' and the same held true with this hour-long exercise.

There was an entire world of activity taking place in just this small area: an ant dragging a dead bug across the ground, to take to the colony. They would live another day, and this ant would be a part of this life. So would the dead bug.

A small breeze, that moved the particles of sand around, just a little bit, but enough to change the landscape of the ground. The trail of the bug being dragged along by the ant was covered up, and one wouldn't even know of such an event happening, except for the observation of it.

The heat of the sun, warming the soil, and some of the particles of the soil actually moving and responding to this heat. Moving. Adjusting. Clearly liking the warmth that the sun was providing.

And along with this wind, a small piece of juniper bark, that would normally go unnoticed, about half an inch in length, and probably five thread-widths across, being at first blown across part of the observation area, and then, coming to rest in a slight 'gully,' having sand being blown in on top of it. Within ten minutes, only a small part of the bark was showing. Minus more heavy winds, or an animal stepping on it and uncovering it again, this piece of juniper bark had served it's purpose, and was now going to feed back in to Mother Earth. Decomposition was sure to be the ultimate outcome. But given the dry nature of the desert, it would spend years decomposing.

When the hour ended, we all gathered together and talked about our observations. The three different levels of what was happening. And how this applied to our own life, our relationships, and to others.

How did our observation impact what was happening. Did anyone do anything to change what was happening in nature? A few had helped an ant along, one had killed the scorpion he found. Another had built up a pile of pebbles, as if nature needed help with creating monuments.

And we talked about this - if they changed the course of nature, in this nine square-foot plot, how? For the better? And an even more important question - how had this nine square-foot plot changed THEM? How would their experience, in this location, at this time, impact them?

Taking a Mental Trip

No, I'm not talking about drugs. I'm talking how the next best thing to being in the wilderness is remembering the wilderness.

Sometimes, and it's happening more and more these days, I find that my sanity is being challenged. Not really sanity, but you know what I mean. It's sometimes almost overwhelming to be in this environment, this society, where we are bombarded with sensory stimulation. Honks, hollers, engines, pollution, stink, doors, people, IPods, phones, artificial light, artificial darkness, soda pop, Internet - the list is endless. Just thinking about all of this raises my blood pressure, I'm sure.

So, how is wilderness my therapy, even in the midst of all this? I take a trip. A trip down memory lane. I go back to the times of a more simple life, a life that I actually lived. A life of not 'roughing it,' but a life of 'living it.' There wasn't fake. There wasn't a constant barrage of input for my attention, begging 'choose me, no - choose me, ..."

In the wilderness, there were still a great many inputs. But these were all *invitations* to listen, to respond, and to actually become a *part of*, and to contribute to, and grow from. In 'civilization,' the stuff that fights for our attention wants to take a little bit of us away. The stuff in the wilderness, on the other hand, offers to help build us, and make us more of who we are and who we want to be. It does this by being a part of us; by leaving a part of itself with us. In civilization, it's more of a 'hit and run.' It takes away, and then leaves. We are less of who we could be, less of who we started out as.

So, when I'm in need of sanity, I take a mental trip. I remember the days when I was young, when I both gave and received, and because of these interactions, everything became a thing of growth.

REPORTING ABUSE

So, from the last week of April to the third week of August, 1989, I slept in a bed about six days total. Actually, I slept in a bed only a day or two, since the other opportunities I had to sleep in a bed were really not comfortable. I'd start out in the bed, but after tossing and turning for 20 minutes, I'd move to the floor. My Momma didn't raise no dummy - I knew when to change spots in life. And so, I'd go to the floor. And then I'd be comfortable, and go to sleep.

My wilderness experience was wonderful.

I learned that, even within hardships, I could find beauty, joy, and peace. Not always pleasure, for sure, but contentment. True contentment.

But, one huge difference between the student's situation and my situation -- I was there voluntarily. They weren't. And because they weren't there voluntarily, there was a 'helpless factor' involved. Add to this some actual negligence that took place, and the situation was not always a pleasant one.

Now, I've read, and nearly memorized, Victor Frankl's book *Man's Search for Meaning*. In it, he rightly states that if a person can find the 'why' for suffering, almost any 'what' can be endured, and even used to grow. In his situation, the abuses were far beyond any that we have experienced in this country. And nothing compared to anything that was experienced in Challenger by anyone, Instructor Abos or Youth Abos.

Nevertheless, when there is neglect or abuse, growing is made harder.

During my time in the desert, there were a few times during the last month of my employment that I was instructed by my boss to 'take cover.' Helicopters would be flying over us on some days, and though I never saw them, I suspected that vehicles were prowling around for our groups as well. I suspected that they were state officials trying to locate our groups, but I don't know this, and didn't then. But I suspected it. What I did know is that we weren't to let any of the individuals in these helicopters see us. It was a big person's game of hide and seek. We would hide; they would seek. Cat and mouse. Modern day Rambo games.

This really got me to thinking about the program.

I had experienced a positive change of heart during my time in the desert. I'd been suicidal earlier in life, and this experience had helped to bring me to the top of the happiness mountain. But as much as it had helped me, I could see and sense that it wasn't doing the same thing for the youth. Not that they weren't benefited by the program. They really were. But there were still some events, and even just the undercurrent of thought and practices, that were harmful to them, and I knew it.

And as much as I was (and am) sold on the wilderness therapy concept, I grew more and more uneasy about some of what occurred at the program.

So, after I left employment in mid-August, I had decided to do something. But I wasn't sure what to do. This I did know - if I didn't do something, I couldn't live with myself when one of the kids was seriously injured or became ill, or even died.

I decided that the best course of action, that would be the most beneficial to the students, would be to inform the attorney general of the state, what I observed and what my experiences were.

In mid-August, I wrote a letter to Jan Graham, the Attorney General for the state of Utah. As I recall, it was five pages long. In it, I detailed as much as I could, my personal experiences in working for the company, and what I personally saw and experienced.

I spoke of withholding water as punishment, which is life-threatening in a desert situation.

I talked about a lack of food. And what to me seemed to be an imbalance of good food.

I told of staff members keeping the youth awake for sometimes 36 or more hours, without any rest.

I told of hikes that went for 20 miles, and nearly 24 hours, without so much as a 30 minute break.

And I had reported to me, though I did not observe, staff telling students to stand at 'attention' whilst others, staff and students, threw fist-sized up to basketball sized rocks towards these students. The crying, the fear to move, and the fear to not move.

These, and other abuses, I detailed in my letter to her.

Now - at this point a disclaimer. I personally did NOT participate in any of these events or activities. They were reported to me by the Young Abos when they came into my section. And since I didn't have the ability to discern if they were being truthful with me or not (I suspected they were, since there was more than one witness to each of the above detailed activities), I reported what I suspected to the Attorney General, and let the law follow up.

The wilderness, Mother Nature, can do much more to teach and change a heart than mankind can ever do. She is impartial. People are not. But she is fair. People are not. When we start to mess with her life-lessons, we end up messing them up.

The best way to utilize the wilderness is to let her lessons be taught without our interference. Sometimes having someone point out, gently and mindfully, the lesson given by Mother Nature is helpful. But a lesson will not be learned if forced upon us, but only if invited. And Mother Nature knows how to invite.

I sent this letter to Jan Graham at the end of August or beginning of September. I don't recall that I ever heard back from her. I may have received a response, but I just don't remember. For all I know, my letter went into one of her fan-mail piles and was never read. But my conscience was clear after I penned the letter.

As I share this experience, my experience, with this particular program, I want to make it absolutely clear that the programs that I am aware of today do not operate with the boot-camp type philosophy. They do NOT abuse children. At least the ones who are members of the Outdoor Behavioral Healthcare Council.

As I mention in another section of this book, I wouldn't hesitate one moment to have one of my children go to any of the programs who are part of this Council. They self-regulate, and do so in order that the public, you and I, can have confidence in them.

Having said this, I would also suggest that if you are considering a wilderness program for a loved one, that you do your due diligence, and explore the program thoroughly. Ask questions, and be discriminating. It is, after all, the well-being of your child that you're talking about.

CURRENT STATE OF WILDERNESS THERAPY

Damage Done Decades Ago

I recently spoke with an individual who, with three others, started a wilderness therapy program in Utah. I shared with him my love for the wilderness, and the power in the wilderness to help us open our eyes to what is really important to us. We really started to connect, *until* I told him that I had worked, years ago, for one of the first wilderness therapy programs. It had it's roots in the survival skills set forth in Larry Dean Olsen's book *Outdoor Survival Skills*, and had as one of the consultants Doug Nelson, the person who started B.O.S.S., or Boulder Outdoor Survival School. He inquired as to the name of the program that I worked for, and I shared it with him - *The Challenger Foundation*, most often shortened to *Challenger*.

At this, his smile turned upside down, and through his frowned faced, told me that the current programs were still fighting the image that *Challenger* left as it's legacy. He said that some great damage and harm were done to the industry because of *Challenger*. And I totally understand. And agree.

When I left *Challenger*, I wrote a five-page letter to then Utah Attorney General Jan Graham, detailing some of my experiences whilst working for *Challenger*, and expressing my concern that though the wilderness therapy concept was indeed life-changing, the way that Challenger was implementiing it was dangerous. I had fears that someone would die in the program. Time proved me right.

My employment ended at *Challenger* in August of 1989. I as there 3 1/2 months as I had planned, then went back to BYU. In 1990, the state of Utah started regulating the programs. But this wasn't soon enough to prevent five deaths, in Utah, that occurred over the next years.

Actually, a 15 year old female was the first person to die in a program. Michelle Sutton of California died in May 1990 whilst enrolled in Summit Quest, based in St. George. One month later, in Jun 1990, a 16 year old female, Kristen Chase of Florida, died of heatstroke, whilst enrolled in Challenger. Steve Cartisano left the state after it was determined that he couldn't participate in any youth programs in-state. He started another company, I think in Hawaii, that was similar in nature to Challenger.

Deaths

In March of 1994 a 16 year old male, Aaron Bacon of Arizona, died of a peritonitis (inflammation of abdominal walls) and a perforated ulcer. Two of the owners of North Star, the program that Aaron died in, were also involved with Challenger.

In January of 2002, Katie Lank of Virginia was hiking near St. George, Utah, and slipped. She fell 70 feet, and was rushed to the hospital. Three weeks later she died in the Las Vegas hospital. The program director Redrock Ranch Academy, settled a lawsuit for a confidential undisclosed amount. This program director worked at Challenger at the same time that I did, and was known for his whistling abilities. He was a kind gentleman, as I remember.

In July of 2002, Ian August of Texas died whilst enrolled in the Skyline Journey program, based out of Nephi, Utah. Two employees, who to my knowledge were never involved with Challenger, were charged with child abuse homicide, but neither person actually went to trial on the charges.

And, nationwide, it is said that there have been over 30 youth who have died in wilderness therapy or adventure therapy programs.

My heart aches for these Young Abos who have lost their lives. So aches.

And for their families. The hole that must be there is possibly inconsolable. In hindsight, would the Young Abo, their parents, the staff and owners of the program, change things? My guess, no - my knowledge is, absolutely!

And yet, even with the tragedy, and the less-significant tragedies, is there still value in wilderness therapy?

Again, my answer is - absolutely.

Outdoor Behavioral Healthcare Council

In 1996, there were some wilderness treatment programs who had the foresight to recognize that their industry would soon be under assault. Therapy is, in and of itself, a risky business. You take a person who is struggling emotionally and / or behaviorally, and do your best to help them self-regulate, and adjust to the society in which they live. But often you are fighting against genetics, culture, sub-cultures, well-meaning but dysfunctional family and friends, non-personal and impersonal policies of schools and places of employment, and therapists and agencies working hard to CYA as a result of litigious people, lawyers, and insurance companies.

Anyway, most people expect therapists and counselors to have 'pixie dust' to fix problems in one session, with no mess. And it just doesn't happen!

Now, add the expectations of 'fixing my son' or 'fixing my daughter,' to also making sure that he or she is safe in the outdoors, filled with bears, snakes, cactus, lack of water, and heights, and you expect Superman to be the counselor.

The battle is uphill to begin with.

So, in 1996 some wilderness therapy agencies got together to create the Outdoor Behavioral Healthcare Council, or OBHC. Their purpose was to keep the focus of the program on the youth being served. To do this, they established guidelines to follow, that spoke to safety, security, expectations of the programs, training of staff, and medical care.

Since 1996, other programs have joined the OBHC, after accepting the stipulations of membership, and the consortium has developed a high respect and regard amongst therapy practitioners in-the-know about wilderness therapy.

From my very outsider-perspective, at this point, it seems that the most successful and highly-regarded programs have 1) disavowed 'boot camp' philosophies as a treatment modality and practice; 2) utilize a positive psychology perspective of individuals, with many of them using the *Arbinger Seminar* and their principles of relationships; 3) do not withhold food, water, and other items required for life; 4) are consistent in their follow-up program, providing counseling to both the youth and his family after the actual wilderness experience is completed.

A Student Experience Recounted

I am friends with a young man who returned from a wilderness therapy program within the past year. With his parent's permission, I sat down with him for over an hour and questioned him, and listened as he volunteered what his experience was like in the program he was in.

Please note a few things before reading this.

First, this is not a sampling of different individuals. This is one individual's experience. What he recounted I am confident is accurate as per his experience. He offered some objective responses as well as some subjective opinions whilst talking with me. I've included both of these in my summary of our conversation.

Second, this is only valid as per his experience in this program. Not all programs are structured the way his was. And whilst this provides a wonderful view into the window of his experience, what he shared with me may not be true of everyone in other programs, or even this very program.

I will call this person 'Ash.' This is part of the name he received whilst in the program.

The program was 13 weeks in length for Ash. He actually graduated a week or two earlier than most students did.

I asked him if the program was good, and he answered emphatically 'Yes.' When I asked him to think about the person he loved the most in this world, and if he would send this person out to the same program he went to, he again offered a resounding 'Yes.' He wouldn't fear for their safety or physical or emotional well-being, he said.

He was NOT a part of the decision to go there. He didn't resist when he was informed by his parents that he would be going, but he was not removed from his home or environment by 'goons.' He went voluntarily. He said that most of the youth WERE removed by either hired escorts, their parents, or others.

Every four days they would receive a food drop. This included hefty portions of rice, oats, dehydrated veggies, and powdered milk. All of them in quart bags. He also said that the youth could earn honey, peanut butter, and cheese. And along with these food drops, fruit was also dropped off.

Also, every four days the youth would talk with a licensed counselor. The groups would hike to a location where a counselor would meet them and talk with them during the food-drop time. Ash said that his counselor was extremely helpful to him. There was a workbook that had components of both primitive skills as well as relationship and mental skills. They would get this signed off at this time.

Food again. There was no killing of any animals. Not even bugs! I was appalled. How did they flavor ash cakes? They were taught how to use plants, but would seldom use plants. They would also try to earn some extra spices. They did have access to salt and pepper all of the time.

They were given toilet paper when they received food. If they needed more, they would use plants: leaves, grasses, etc.

Every week they would be able to 'sponge bathe.' And every two weeks they were required to shower. One of those camp showers, with an attendant enclosure, would be brought in. At the same time, they would receive a fresh shirt and socks. The pants they kept the entire time. And all of their clothing was issued by the company. Nothing came from home.

They had two pair of footwear. A pair of hiking boots, that they only wore whilst hiking, and a pair of croc-like shoes. When they got to camp, they had to pile up their hiking boots, and wear the crocs. This was to make sure that their opportunity to run was cut down, with the footwear they had on.

They slept in a group shelter at night. Good behavior would earn them a chance to sleep outside of the shelter on a groundcloth. This really was a reward, as per Ash. Because sleeping in the shelter was stuffy and, well, full of boys and boy smell.

The groups were NOT co-ed. The staff sometimes included a female, but never were any of the students female in a male group, and vice versa.

The groups consisted of anywhere from 3-9 people each, and whilst Ash was in the field, there were four groups most of the time. When he left the program, I think he said that there may have been six groups.

There were three phases, or what I called sections.

The first was when the youth worth a survival pack. They could earn a regular backpack, but most didn't for the first three or four weeks. By the second section, most of the youth had a backpack, and it was good. The third section was also a 'backpack' section.

Psychologically, there was no shaming. There were hardships, and consequences, but Ash said that he never felt picked on or emotionally abused or neglected. Rather, he said, there were a few people who really encouraged him, and helped him want to be better.

About four weeks prior to his graduation, Ash went through the naming ceremony. Again, for most this usually happened more towards the end, but for Ash it was a full month before he left the program.

They would also get 'knifed.' To earn a knife, they would have to not run, show no aggression towards others or self, and to have no history of self-harm.

Of particular interest to me was the 101 Firepatch. For a youth who had started 101 fires, he or she earned a Firepatch. Ash attached his patch to his medicine bag, around his neck. Of continued interest, when Ash left the program, he had the record of starting over 400 fires with primitive methods, mostly with a bow drill, but some with handdrill and a pump drill.

I asked what his favorite bow-drill set was. He said he especially liked a juniper fireboard and a sage spindle. If they were ever around yucca, this was his preferred, but in the area he was in, yucca wasn't that prevalent.

The manual that they had, with the lessons inside, were a combination of primitive skills and relationship skills. The primitive stuff included such things as Camp set-up, shelter construction, firepit construction, constellations, plants, animal tracks and poop, and glue.

Ash said that flint knapping was voluntary, but that he did it.

They would get as much water, and more, than they wanted. Mostly is was from water barrels that would be refilled on a regular basis. Occasionally they would use horse troughs and other, more natural sources.

Ash said that 8 to 10 times a day, the staff would call 'half quart.' The youth would then be required to show staff their water bottles, drink half a quart of water, then show the staff that it was half gone. The company was taking no chances of dehydration. Good, good precaution!

Ash's father said that Ash came back from the program more healthy than when he left. He lost weight and became more fit and 'cut.'

Did I mention that there was usually two staff with each group of 8, but sometimes there was three staff.

To summarize the whole experience, Ash said it was like a 'Cosmic slap in the face.' The program helped him to realize that if a student was succeeding, it was their problem. However the program did it, and the staff, Ash came away knowing that he goes forward or backward in life based upon his own decisions.

Digging a Bit Deeper

As I was about wrapping up the writing of this book, and feeling to pat myself on the back, I spoke with a few other folks who have experience in working as counselors for wilderness therapy programs in the early days. And this was enlightening to me.

It seems that many of the early programs actually did come with a set of operation standards that weren't that far off of what Challenger operated from as well. I guess that this would stand to reason, given that the *modus operandi* in almost any industry tends to follow the same bell curve. So that, if a wilderness therapy, or outdoor therapy program were to start up today, it would be operated within the same general parameters as the others are. Oh, there are exceptions - I know. But take for example Tesla. It pushes the limits of vehicle ingenuity, but hey, they're still cars.

This particular individual with whom I spoke recounted an experience in her employment with a company (she was working for one of the better programs, with a good reputation, and where nobody has died) where she was lost, with another employee, and two students, without water, and had to dig. A very similar experience to mine. And it wasn't the same company that I worked for, but about the same time.

At any rate, hearing this, then reading and putting together the experience of Bill, whose story is in the B*ack Matter* of this book, leads me to the realization, or rather suspicion, that the various programs at the onset of this industry were quite similar in nature, and it was over the years that they evolved in reaction to 1) lawsuits, 2) the deaths in the programs, and 3) a greater understanding of student safety.

All Change Comes with a Cost

Whenever a change is made, and a different course pursued, one gives up some possibilities and inherits other possibilities. The changes that have occurred over the years in the wilderness therapy concept and implementation have proven to be safe changes. The litigation has been minimized in the programs. Student and staff safety is a high priority now, and in fact is probably the top priority. Both of these are good changes. The lawyers of today's world get way too much of our hard-earned dollars, so any time that law suits can be kept out of the hands of the attorney's, I'm happy. And they're not! And that's OK with me.

But the changes have come about with a price, in my opinion. Some of the very risks, the very activities, that I participated in through my wilderness therapy experience are those that had the most profound impact and change on me. And it's really hard to quantify exactly what this impact is, but it's real.

Nobody died on my shift. I guess part of the reason is good luck. But part of the reason is because *we were safe (minus going into the desert without water) even though it was hard.* Hardship doesn't mean unsafe. And what I see happening today, which is really only a gut feeling, is that hardships are being removed from the programs. Why? I don't know.

Whiners? Possibly. Being overly cautious? Probably. I know that most medical organizations now are given a set of rules that they need to abide by. But many of these organizations, at least the big ones, will then impose their OWN rules on the workers, which are more restrictive than the law requires. This is to avoid litigation. But, really, I see this as hurting both patient care as well as increasing the cost of patient care.

Some examples that I think would be safe, but be much more effective in a good wilderness therapy program:

Scrap the sleeping bags! Go back to tarps and blankets.

Use food-safe cans rather than camp cups.

Teach the Young Abos traps, and *have them use them to procure food.*

Make shelters, low-impact methods, rather than use tents.

Have sheep and chicken-kills. Teach the Young Abos a reverence for life, and also how to prepare food from the beginning.

Take the parents on the trail for three or more days. (I'm not sure that this ever happened, but in many of these dysfunctional relationships, the parents are as much of the solution [and the problem] as the Young Abos.)

Some ways that I feel that the programs have improved over the years:

Satellite Phones and other electronic devices used to call for help.

OBHC oversight for the programs.

As a licensed clinical social worker, I can say with the highest degree of confidence that I would, today, not hesitate to recommend any client to any wilderness therapy program associated with the Outdoor Behavioral Healthcare Council. As a father, I can also confidently say that I would not fear for the safety, physically or emotionally, of my child in any of these same programs. There are some whose philosophies more closely align with my personal philosophy of human nature and change, but as far as safety is concerned, I have no fears.

ACKNOWLEDGEMENTS

I ought to acknowledge some folks here who really don't fit in anywhere else, but in truth, fit everywhere.

My wife, Christine. For allowing and supporting my occasional backcountry trips. Sometimes with some of my children, sometimes alone. And for also allowing my periods of ruminating at home, when I'm not able to get into the backcountry. And for attending the primitive skills groups and trainings with me (occasionally).

My children, for allowing me the same freedoms as their mother.

My parents, for supporting me in Scouts. Dad, who has since passed on, was never really in very good shape, but allowed, and arranged, for others to take me outdoors. John Zito, Chuck Gividen, Earnie Hammer, Grandpa, Leonard Zito, and others.

My progenitors who helped to settle the Bitterroot Valley, Montana. A story is in the making for them and their contributions. Pioneers they were, in the Salish and Lewis and Clark country, and sung about by John Denver in *Wild Montana Skies*. This is my home. This, and the Bob Marshall Wilderness.

For my junior high teacher, Mrs. Eden, for setting a base for writing. I'm not sure if she'll like this style or not, however. Thanks anyway! For my high school teacher, who will remain unnamed, for giving me a 'D,' and telling me that I would never amount to anything as a writer, and the only reason that he didn't give me an 'F,' is because it would reflect poorly upon him as a teacher. To my two English professors at Ricks College, who both gave me an 'A,' and who independently and sincerely expressed amazement at my writing skills, and encouraged me to continue writing. It only took about 15 years for this to sink in!

To the Young Abos with whom I had the privilege to work.

To Ash and his family. Thanks for the hours you spent sharing your experiences with me.

To my God, to whom I am forever and deeply indebted and hold in awe, for the creative artwork of this earth.

MAJOR PLAYERS IN WILDERNESS THERAPY PROGRAMS

There have been, I'm guessing, over three dozen outdoor therapy programs, wilderness therapy programs, outdoor adventure programs, or something along those lines, since the 1980's. Possibly many more - someone please correct me if I'm wrong (thefigproject@gmail.com). Some of the early one's seemed to be based more on the 'boot camp' philosophy. Thankfully, all of these have gone out of business, to my knowledge. And thankfully, these were a large minority of such programs.

Most of the present programs are based upon a strengths model, meaning that rather than focus on the problems of a person, they focus on helping the person to change by encouraging strengths. This is the better way to elicit more positive and lasting change.

Challenger, the program that I worked for, was one of the first wilderness therapy programs. Many good people worked for this program. But the program was flawed from the beginning due to the 'boot camp' philosophy that was utilized as the change agent. I worked for Challenger during the Summer of 1989. I don't know how long it was in existence prior to this time.

The **Anasazi Foundation**, founded in 1988 by Larry Dean Olsen and Ezekiel Sanchez, operated on a wholly different philosophy than did Challenger. Using the 'strengths' approach, Anasazi is celebrating their 30 year anniversary this year, 2018. I have had occasion to visit with Ezekiel (Zeke, or Good Buffalo Eagle), and some of the other employees of Anasazi, and find their approach to be both safe and liberating. Without hesitation, I have recommended for students and families to participate in Anasazi.

Another 'ancient' program, **Red Cliffs Ascent**, has been around since the 1990's. They seem to share a similar philosophy as Anasazi. The are also a founding member, along with Anasazi, of the Outdoor Behavioral Healthcare Council.

As a counselor, I look at a few things when I make a referral to any resource. As far as wilderness programs are concerned, I look to see that they are a safe program. What is their track record? Injuries? Deaths? Circumstances?

I look at their treatment philosophy. If they are going to manipulate or treat the youth as if they are deficient, I will not refer. Of course, youth are deficient. Or else they wouldn't be going to therapy - right?! But hey, don't treat the Young Abos this way. Give them a vision of who they are, and then give them the tools to get there!

I look at self-policing. Frankly, I don't trust that the government has either the resources to police the programs, or the understanding to do so. So, if the programs make up their standards, share what these standards are with others, then hold each other accountable for maintaining these standards, this is the best way to be.

That is why I am totally comfortable with the Outdoor Behavioral Healthcare Council. They have standards that they have all committed to abide by, and hold each other accountable. They want to maintain safety as well as the confidence of the public. Good, good move in my book.

Now, for anyone looking to utilize or use a wilderness treatment program, do your homework. Look at their website. Read what past parents and participants have said. It is not just tens of thousands of dollars that are at stake. It is the life of your child, and your family relationship.

One last word of caution - you will find naysayers. Some folks just want to muddy the waters. They offer no productive thoughts, and only want to upset and discourage. Don't listen to them. If their goal is to dissuade you from treatment in the outdoors, write them off as agitators, and not builders.

MAJOR PLAYERS IN WILDERNESS THERAPY

There are some folks who have played a major role in wilderness therapy. But first, a disclaimer.

Being in the wilderness is therapy, in and of itself. All folks who have worked in any sort of outdoor program that takes folks into the wilds will know this. Well, the insightful ones will.

So, when I list a few of the major players in this field, I do so knowing that this list is wholly incomplete. I surely don't mean to offend anyone by leaving them off this list. And this is why I've limited this list to those 'fathers' of the business.

Larry Dean Olsen

He started, along with Ezekiel 'Zeke' Sanches, the Anasazi Foundation, typically just called Anasazi. But even before this, wilderness therapy was started back in the 1960's at Brigham Young University. Some of the students who were struggling were given the opportunity to go on a trip to the desert (Butch Cassidy country), and through this experience, their sense of self reawakened, and they came back to continue their college studies. This was the real beginning of this field.

Ezekiel 'Zeke' Sanchez

He was one of the first students of Larry Olsen's at BYU. The transformation set him on a course that would impact the rest of his life.

On a personal note, Zeke is one of the only people who I have walked into the same room as he was in, and felt wrapped up in acceptance from him. For spiritual folks, he exudes a love and encouragement that I've felt in only a handful of people.

Doug Nelson

Doug, who was a BYU survival program student in the early days, started one of the very first companies, Aspen Achievement Academy, to provide an actual psychotherapeutic experience. This was a flagship program, which he later sold. Doug went on to teach survival skills at BYU.

When I took an introductory wilderness survival course at BYU in the 1990's, I took the course from Doug.

MAJOR PLAYERS IN PRIMITIVE SKILLS

This is a section that could literally fill a book. In fact, this is the section that nearly put a stop to this book. I started working on this chapter, and it kept getting bigger, and bigger, and bigger. I started to get discouraged, realizing that this was going to take more time, energy, effort, and more of everything, than I really wanted to give to it.

So, I cut WAY back.

For future reference, I would recommend that some ambitious soul take the project upon themselves to write a book on the recent history of the rebirth of primitive skills. There are gatherings, knap-ins, workshops, classes, and businesses built around this. And it's expanding. I'd buy the book. It would make for a fascinating read.

So, I've decided to include in this chapter 16 individuals. Some of them are here because they are authors. Some are TV show hosts or stars. Some are YouTube stars. Some are my friends. All are educators. Nobody is here because I've been paid to have him or her here. All names, and people, are legit.

In alphabetical order, these are some of the major players of the past, some present major players, and some up-and-coming players, in the field of primitive skills. It is not comprehensive. If you've been left off the list, please let me know who you are, and if a second edition comes out, I'll put you on it. Or let me know of someone else who ought to be on this list.

If you would like to take on the project of completing a whole new book, filled with the primary players in primitive skills, I'd be happy to collaborate and assist.

Brown, Tom: Author. The 'father' of primitive skills and living on the East Coast.

Canterbury, Dave: A TV personality, YouTube star, and former cast member of Dual Survival, along with Cody Lundin. Author of some great books on survival and primitive skills.

Farnamen, Cat: The guru when it comes to herbs and medicinal plants. All around good person, who would put any doc to shame when it comes to healing.

Farnamen, Patrick: Started the gathering *Between the Rivers* in Washington state. A fellow *social worker* and adventurer. I've never met the guy, but he's got a zest for life that is contagious.

Graham, Matt: An expert atlatl practitioner. BOSS school graduate as well as instructor. A long-distance runner, reality TV show star, and host of *Bushcraft Buildoff.*

Holliday, David: The man who lives what he knows. Read Larry Dean Olsen's book years ago, and put into practice that which he learned.

Storyteller and straight-up good person. His oddity is inspiring, as is his goodness. When I grow up, I want to be more like him.

Kochanski, Mors: A Canadian survivor and practitioner of primitive skills and camping skills. Cody Lundin considers Mors his mentor, or one of them.

Lundin, Cody: Former TV star. Former BOSS student and employee. Owns and operates a school of wilderness survival. Author of two of the best books on survival and preparedness available. Hands down, he is a no-BS guy who shoots as straight as anyone I've ever read. Interested in telling the truth, and not in filling books with fluff.

Magleby, Kelly: On Facebook as Ki Kayenta. Mentored by John Olsen. Together, they know more about Anasazi pottery, and how to recreate it, than all of the textbooks and articles written on the subject. Kelly graciously gave permission for two of her photographs from an expedition into the wild deserts of Southern Utah to be used in this book.

Nelson, Doug: Started BOSS, Boulder Outdoor Survival Skills. BYU Professor in survival skills. A founder of the wilderness therapy model.

Olsen, Larry Dean: The grandfather of the movement. Started at BYU, and then he started the Anasazi Foundation with Zeke Sanchez. Wrote

Outdoor Survival Skills, which is the premier text on survival skills. No library is complete without this.

Powell, Lord Baden: Started the Boy Scouts of America. Possibly the great grandfather of outdoor skills. Not necessarily a primitive skills enthusiast, but has been responsible for getting millions of people back to the outdoors.

Stewart, Creek: A former boy scout. TV personality. Author. Superb wilderness survival instructor and enthusiast, who is grounded as a Christian. I'm very impressed by him. So are thousands of others.

Wade, Brad: Started the gathering *Fire to Fire* near Tabiona, Utah. Binding journals primitively is his specialty, but he knows enough in a dozen areas to be considered a master instructor. For one week in June, the 200 acres near Tabiona has more people on it than in the town! Some of the best in primitive skills are present for this down-home, rub shoulders, gathering. An article written about *Fire to Fire* will be printed in the outdoor magazine *The Backwoodsman*, written by yours truly!

Larry Wells: Taking what he learned as an inmate in the Idaho State Penitentiary, Larry started a program for wayward youth. He is also considered one of the grandfather's of wilderness therapy.

Wescott, Dave: Second owner of BOSS. Found (or was found by) and hired David Holliday at BOSS. BYU-Idaho instructor, and founder of Rabbitstick, the oldest primitive skills gathering in the US.

KENDRA DAVIS' EXPERIENCE

Whilst perusing the Internet one September day in 2018, I came across an article from BYU, mentioning Kendra's name. She had participated in the BYU survival program sometime in the 20-teens. I don't know the year.

But I wrote to her anyway, and asked if I could include her experience in this book. She said yes, and emailed to me the her experience.

This is a summary of Kendra Davis' experience whilst on a four-day BYU survival trip. I found a story about Kendra at:

https://jesslikesjournalism.com/wilderness-trek-could-your-survive-it/

After going on the program as a student, she then went out as a TA.

A big thank you to Kendra for sharing this.

****

Last weekend was hands down the hardest four days of my life. I was pushed to my limits and found out I can rise to that challenge. Going out I was worried if I could even do it all. I knew I could make a shelter, I knew I wasn't going to die or anything stupid like that but I was worried that I'd let myself down. While I was nervous about not getting a fire my first night, or even at all, what really stressed me out was that mentally I would break. The second night out there I really wanted to quit. I was cold, tired, hungry, and my thoughts were trying to put me into a dark place. I don't know what time it was exactly, but the sun had been down for hours. I navigated my way to base camp by moonlight and told Jake what was going on. I told him I didn't want to quit but I needed help getting through this rough patch. He made me some Brigham's Tea and I sat by the fire for a bit and we talked until I could get back in control of my thoughts and then Jake helped me navigate back to my site. I crawled into my sleeping bag and finally got some rest. I woke up in the morning and felt ready to tackle the rest of the final with way more confidence than I had the day before. Whenever I got down on myself I would think back to my talk with Jake at the campfire and it would shut down my negative thinking. That's when I started to believe that I could actually do hard things. The rest of the final went by quickly and it was much more enjoyable than the first half and I look back at the weekend as a positive event overall. [I go more into detail about the final but details on what happens on the final are kept confidential since not knowing what will happen is a big part of the experience, I would hate to spoil it for future members of the course] I'm excited for class this week so we can talk more about the final, I'm curious how everyone else felt about it. We were all exhausted when we headed home so we all slept in the vans the whole way back. Jake mentioned that anyone who completes the class can come back and TA, I'm thinking that might be a fun idea. I'd like to do more of this. Braden [TA for that semester and now a very good friend of mine] seems to enjoy it, he's been doing it for three semesters.

BILL BARLOW'S EXPERIENCE

In September of 2018, whilst perusing the Internet searching for all things related to survival programs, I came across this journal entry, posted by one Bill Barlow, on Facebook. I read with great interest his experience in 1974, and thought that, if he was willing, I would like to include his experience in this book.

I sent him a Messenger message explaining my project, and asked if he would be Ok if I included his experience in my book. He responded positively.

I then realized that I couldn't copy his text from his Facebook post, so I emailed him again, and asked if he would have access to this in a different format, that he could email to me. He graciously replied, and I was able to cut and paste his experience here.

I have not made any corrections. For the sake of easing the read, I have bolded some text. Other than this, it remains unchanged from how he sent it to me.

Thank you Bill.

*****   *****   *****   *****   *****

BYU Survival Program: 1974 Trip

Bill B <tohopko@yahoo.com.ph>

The following is about my 'Tough Trip Through Paradise". That name is taken from my favorite book of the same name, taken from the pages of Andrew Garcia's memoirs, and made into my favorite movie, 'Little Big Man'.

My 'tough trip' was 28 days of a BYU survival course through south east and south central Utah during May and June 1974. My journal entries are updated with information in parenthesis, added later to better describe things.

During my time at BYU, my housemates and I found some female students who would cook supper for us in return for money for food. Two of them, Carol Jensen and Lynn Kanavel, were past participants of the BYU Survival program. Their stories intrigued me and eventually I changed my major to Youth Leadership, which included the requirement of BYU Survival. I got very close to the four female roommates and Carol thought it would be fun to go on Survival again to watch me experience it for the first time. My girlfriend at that time, Sherry Cook, also decided to go.

Way in advance of the trip, all participants were advised to buy comfortable hiking boots and wear them for several months prior so their feet and boots were broken in. One of the best decisions I ever made was to follow that advice.

The only things we were able to take with us was one wool army blanket, personal health care items, a can to drink out of and cook in, a canteen, a coat and sweater, and rope to tie it all together wrapped up in the blanket. We were really going to rough it.

We boarded the bus and drove to our drop-off point, and before getting there we were advised to drink as much water as we could. I couldn't get beyond about 12 soda cans full, but some drank much more. Needless to say, the last 20 miles of the trip was interrupted by numerous potty breaks, girls to the right of the bus, guys to the left.

The first 3 days of the trip were called 'Impact'. We were to leave everything on the bus except our coats and sweaters and our drinking can. No blanket, no personal grooming things, no canteen. These would be waiting for us at a pre-determined location at the end of our hike. Oh yeah, no food either. It was May 9th and we hiked down into a large dry wash canyon that I believe was 'Horseshoe Canyon'.

Tough Trip Through Paradise

My Diary, Parenthesis added after the trip:

May 10 (Friday morning, 1974)

We just woke up. We slept on the sand without a blanket and it got a little cool. All of the guys ended up around the fire. Yesterday we traveled about 8 miles for our first day. (We did have a topo map) We're in a beautiful canyon where a river sometimes flows, but not now. Quite a few of the 28 (?) people are getting blisters. (28 students and 4 instructors) Lots of Indian pictographs from Anasazi Indians about 800 years ago. Don't feel any hungrier yet than yesterday, but we won't get food till Saturday night.

Friday night:

We just had a super hard day. Covered about 12 miles and was very hungry - still no food. Many more have blisters and many have upset stomachs. (The only water we found was a pothole with many cow tracks around and in the water... also cow poop. Most filtered the water through their bandannas) Talk of different kinds of food dominates. My problem was I was really tired. All the guys bedded down in a damp place and it was cold out anyway, so we all froze and got almost no sleep. Either got too close or too far away from the fire, and the ground was hard. Toward night, my hunger faded.

(Carol gave me some candy she had smuggled on the trip)

Saturday, May 11

We got up this morning at 4:30 after a very sleepless night. (Instructors sleep away from us with all the niceties of a typical backpacker, including food and clean water) Still have a lot of upset stomachs and 2 people puked. We had to hike 10-12 miles (more) for our 1st weekend base-camp where we finally got some food. Good - raw oatmeal and brown sugar. (And wheat flour, one cup of each) We're having stew. (Potatoes, carrots and Texturized Vegetable Protein - TVP) They still don't give you very much to live on, particularly on weekdays I hear. It sure is nice to eat and relax. Everyone really appreciates food.

Sunday, May 12

Made a coal-bed to sleep on (last night) and it's good I did. (I have been studying survival for a while now) It was really cold last night. (Everyone was freezing even with their coats and army blanket on) I woke up sweating a couple times. (Instructors told me no more coal beds as it sterilizes the ground. True, but I think they didn't want me that comfortable either) Had a Mother's Day Sunday service today and it was very good and spiritual. The guys all collected wildflowers and gave them to the girls.

Had stew for supper, ash cakes with brown sugar inside, hamburgers, WOW!

*Note to self - Make oatmeal, brown sugar, raisins etc, and pour natural peanut butter over it and put in refrigerator. (This begins the shared and made up recipes that dominated most of our thoughts and conversation)

Slept with a few girls - a no-no, but they had a warmer spot.

Monday, May 13

Got a late start for Robbers Roost. (Butch Cassidy and his gang used this area as a getaway and sanctuary. Their old fireplace and chimney is still there) Beautiful place, specially the canyon, narrow cliffs and steep. We're in 'Group Expedition' now, (for the next week) 6 guys, 1 instructor, and a photographer and a writer for BYU and 'Camping Magazine'. I've been assigned to cook so far. I'm pretty good and no one is too smart as to how much etc. (ingredients) But at least I get out of (cleaning) dishes and I get to clean the pot out. Dinner - Lentil, Brown rice, carrots, TVP stew.

Tuesday, May 14

Had a great night's sleep. One group of guys ahead of us and 2 groups of girls somewhere behind. But the girls are really trucking and if we don't break camp they'll be coming.

(The 5 or 6l hour trip down Robbers Roost Canyon was very tough, but at least down hill. Each group had use of a climbing rope and we had to use them a couple times to get down steep areas. The canyon was one of those that you wouldn't want to be in during a thunderstorm because of flash flood potential. Several areas we could not see the sky for the overhanging cliffs, and one spot we could barely squeeze through sideways)

We're out of the canyon now and in the canyon of the Dirty Devil. (River) A lot of us now are dragging. I am tired but others are not keeping up. Got my first blister but it's small and not bad. Rick got stuck in quicksand up to his waist. Hairy! (One student was closest to him but as soon as he felt the pull of the quicksand himself, he turned and walked away, leaving Larry I believe to pull Rick out)

Food for the week - cracked wheat, powdered milk, flour, brown sugar, TVP, honey, Bullion cubes, 2 carrots, oatmeal, brown rice, and lentils.

Tonight a ranger hiked in and put on a program. Country legends, and music. The boys from the other section came in.

(There were actually two sections of about 30 people from BYU out there at the same time. They had their own instructors and route they would take, and this was the only time during the 28 days that we would cross paths. I'm guessing the instructors had a great time comparing notes on their students hardships. We hardly ever see the instructors as they keep to themselves for preciously stated reasons... the food, the tent, the sleeping bags, the strippers, etc. Just kidding about that last one)

Wednesday, May 15

We were allowed to sleep late since we're waiting for the girls from the other section. So we did, got up at 7:30! Washed my upper body and 2 pairs of socks and that always feels good. It's unbelievable how we sleep, sand or dirt for a pillow, sand all over and oblivious to it, like pigs in a poke. Larry and I slept together (last night) and we were warm. But it was our warmest night too.

(Larry Nelson and I just kind of bonded during this adventure. He was a PE jock and Rugby player with the looks of the Marlboro Man. He carried the heavy climbing rope and other people's blanket packs when they were having trouble. Simply put, he was amazing)

We're going to hold over probably most or all of today, and then we have 50 miles to do

Thursday and Friday to get into base camp at the Henry Mountains. (Waiting for those girls to show up screwed us out of another day to travel and we'll pay the price big time soon)

We're now at the mouth of Beaver Wash on the Dirty Devil, had cracked wheat for breakfast. Joey Armstrong (gave everyone her address in San Diego and invited anyone to come and stay) The rest of the day was slow and lazy. Carol is really acting -not herself- and she won't talk to me cause I guess she knows it too. Sherry is running out of things to talk about, me too. Had a fireside with skits and songs.

(This was where I had my first bowel movement since the 8th of May. I get that way during trips, but at least I didn't have the problem others had after drinking out of cow tracks)

Thursday, May 16

Good night's sleep. Tim Lemmon, a buddy from Section 2 slept with me and Larry and gave us some raisins. Finally going to get out of this sand for a change. First we're going to learn some skills, then trek. We're really going to have a long way to travel.

It's 8PM and what an interesting day! I was picked as leader for my section(of our 28 people) and with the leader of the other section, it was our job to lead about 56 people over unbelievable country.

(I was the only guy in our section who was essentially in training for survival and had been because of the major of Youth Leadership I was taking. I'm guessing this had some impact on the instructors decision to pick me to lead what was to be the most difficult two days of the trip. I think they wanted to see if I could handle it)

We started out bush-whacking up Beaver Creek and then up and out of the Canyon, climbing out over really high bluffs. We had to set up a rope to help, it was fairly steep but wildest of all, there was a 50 MPH wind up on the hills with gusts that must have gone to 80. We got on top and had about 4 miles of sandy, dirt road with the wind in our faces, only about 25 MPH now. We made it to a water drop here at Pool Springs. In a couple hours, about 10-11 PM, we'll be off again in a nighttime hike toward weekend camp in the Henrys.

Friday, May 17

Well last night when we finally took off, it was about 11, pitch dark and I led again. We walked 11 more miles which made 19 for the day. We got to our destination at 4:15 in the morning, (Wind swept, bare ground, still short of our weekend camp in the Henry Mountains) and we got up at 8:00 (AM) and walked about 10 more to weekend base camp. That night walk was a bear, everyone was exhausted and I had to really fight to keep them going. A couple fell asleep while they walked. (going off the trail) I felt great, but the next morning was terrible. (less than 4 hours sleep, up since Thursday morning, walked 19 miles and then 10 more to go that morning. I don't know how many miles I walked Thursday night because I was back and forth along our group that was strung out maybe a quarter mile or more, encouraging as best I could those who didn't think they could go any farther)

The instructors planned it that way on purpose and it worked. Everyone was exhausted, never been so tired.

(Part of the trip was designed to break us down physically and mentally, but the instructors were a bit frustrated because our group was helping each other and doing so well. Survival was designed to help Juvenile delinquents get over their self reliance, reach the end of their rope and realize they needed to accept authority and learn to work together to survive. Kinda like boot camp)

We made base camp. Larry and I made a lean-to out of old boards we found and ate with Sherry and Jo. Sure is nice to be at base camp. Tomorrow we kill a sheep and eat it.

Saturday, May 18

Not a very good night for sleep last night. Too cold. (We were on a bench of the Henrys at higher altitude than we had been) Tonight we'll have a fire and more clothes on, every stitch I own. Had cracked wheat - cooked- for breakfast, sure like it. We all gathered together for the sheep kill. A girl volunteered to shoot it behind the ear while me and two others held it down. Then we prepared it, all of it, intestines and all. Jerked a lot and had sheep stew for supper. Someone stole my brown sugar from me today; I have a hunch who it was; have to keep an eye on them. Looks like it might rain tonight, ugh. I'm glad we did the sheep, now I know how to prepare a big animal.

Sunday, May 19

Slept better but it was still cold and windy. Gave a talk in church today on Success, Happiness, and Hardships. Had fried sheep lung for supper.

*Recipe - cornmeal added to flour for ash cakes, also brown sugar, water and grated orange rind makes great syrup for everything, also orange grated in the pancakes. (Now if we only had pancakes!)

Monday, May 20

Last night was absolutely freezing. Carol came over and slept with me and Larry, and she was warmer but she took up most of the fire. I just noticed that most of the hair is burned off my hands. Everyone's hands really take a beating out here. This base camp is at Lost Springs, about 25 miles south of Hanksville, just on the west side of the Henry Mountains. Looks like excellent deer hunting with a good road and hopefully few hunters. Many deer sign. Found a great 4 point rack still on the skull. We had a few snowflakes fall today! Deer season closed! We played intuitive tests today and our group did really well, best in fact. (ok, so I'm competitive and Larry and I made a great team)

The weather has warmed up a little but tonight we'll see. I'm reading The Hobbit now, pretty interesting. Larry invited me up to his ranch north of Sun Valley. His folks have 400 acres up there. Be sure to check into graduate school at Michigan State and the Masters in Outdoor Education. Also check the Post Office as soon as I get back for a job this Summer term! Finish everything this Fall semester. (Did)

Tuesday, May 21

Well it wasn't windy last night and it was beautiful, but it was pretty cold again. Fitful sleep. This sleep in the dirt, sit in the dirt, eat in the dirt, is just amazing. I washed my face today and then looked in a mirror. My skin was still dirty.

Well we're packing up to leave on 'Survival Week' now. The instructors painted a pretty harsh picture of it last night. I think we'll be very weak from lack of food soon.

Wednesday, May 22

Had a short 5-7 mile hike, all uphill, and are now at 7,600 feet. Was very cold last night and hard sleeping. Estimate about 37-38 degrees last night. Tonight we will be at about 8,600 feet and colder no doubt.

Well we're here, this is a beautiful place, still on the Henrys. We finish up our food tonight, then we go pretty much without until Sunday. We're halfway to the end now.

Thursday, May 23

La Morena Cafe in the Guadupele Center near the Salt Palace is supposed to be good Mexican food. (It was very good)

*Sandwich- Peanut butter, sour cream, honey, bananas. *Chocolate chip dough pressed into brownies. *Toasted - peanut butter, tuna and cheese. Also Carol's tuna with mustard, cottage cheese, etc etc. *Also oatmeal and Peanut Butter and honey or brown sugar, and anything else, pressed into a pan and heated in oven, or use granola, not oatmeal... and chocolate bits and marshmallow. *Lumpy Dick - powdered milk - boil almost and dump in flour. Bullion cubes too, and onion. spice. Good over ash cakes or potatoes.

(Yes, I really did write down the recipes all these people were passing around or just verbalizing)

Hiked 10 miles today, got a couple ash cakes each at a food drop. We're back in the desert now and I hope it will be warmer tonight. Lots of clouds in the sky, hope it doesn't rain.

Friday, May 24

Had a good sleep and a handful of lettuce for breakfast, and then set out for base camp 7 miles away. Really weak as was everyone, and sore leg muscles. But we're here (base camp) and being threatened with rain. One girl is so hungry she is licking her cherry flavored Lip Saver. Just finished reading The Hobbit. I've really lost a lot of weight. I can see it in my arms and legs and I think my chest.

Saturday, May 25

Fast Day; slow, beautiful day. *Check on a thyroid slower. I loose weight faster than anyone I think.

(I can laugh now. 2 ash cakes Thursday, a handful of iceberg lettuce on Friday, and today is FAST DAY??? Are you kidding me!!!)

Sunday, May 26 (Fast Sunday)

*Taco shells, refried beans and deep fried for burrito, also not filled with lettuce, tomato, etc.

Today we were really weak, could hardly walk but the instructor came in and we had church which lasted 2 3/4 hours - Fast and Testimony meeting. It was really good. Then we had dinner finally. We started out with oatmeal that was very good to us, then I had an orange - great! Then we had cabbage, potato and onion soup. Then I had chicken, 4 pieces, a leg, a thigh, a back and a breast. Also about 2 1/2 glasses of milk. I'm stuffed. Oh yeah, another can of cabbage, potato, onion stew.

(I should add here that it was pretty windy and sand got blown into the oatmeal pot that still had oatmeal in it, lots of sand. It was very gritty, but hey. As Uncle Si would say)

Now we have to rest up and about 1 AM, we leave on our 27-30 mile hike. Hope to get in by about noon tomorrow.

(We were told it was a sort of competition, we could not run but we could walk very fast)

*Bread pudding - cook milk, 4 cups, not quite boil. Beat up 4 eggs and 1/4 cup butter. Vanilla, teaspoon - 1 or 2, and raisins and cinnamon. Whole wheat bread, broken up until micture is almost soaked up. Cook in pan or casserole dish. Bake 350 for about an hour. - can add nuts, chocolate, etc. * Graham cracker crushed in bottom of pan, pour in half cup butter on top, add cup of coconut and either chocolate or butterscotch chips, and walnuts, and pour can of sweet condensed milk, and bake 350 for 20 minutes.

Monday, May 27

Well it's Monday afternoon and we've all been resting. We started our 26 mile hike at 12:30 AM this morning. Larry, Steve and I gravitated to the front even though I felt weak. Once I got moving I was better. We went most of the way together but the last mile and a half, Steve dropped back. (We were walking very fast the whole time) Larry and I ran the last hundred yards and crossed first. (finish line, holding hands) Our time was 6 hours and 40 minutes. I was really hurting most of the way but so was everyone. I got my first bothersome blister and a sore spot.

(Due to my usual constipation and trying my hardest to strain something out, I got a painful hemorrhoid a week ago. Walking always bothered it but this very fast walking for more than 6 hours made it exceptionally painful. In order to lessen the discomfort during our 'forced march', I would occasionally reach into my pants with my cherry flavored lip saver – CFLS, and lubricate said hemorrhoid. Sometime during the night, while walking, I dropped the tube of lip saver. I must explain here that CFLS was one of those items that you just didn't want to be without, literally worth its weight in gold, or maybe even diamonds. Not only did our dry, sunburned lips need it so badly, our constant, starving condition was given a sweet waft of heavenly manna whenever anyone popped the top on their CFLS tube. Although unfortunate for me at the time, this loss proved to be very significant which will be explained near the end of my 'Tough Trip' narrative)

We start out on 'Student Expedition' tomorrow where we have to cover 70-80 miles in 4 days. So really the worst is over. The rest will be kinda fun.

(If somehow you haven't grasped the difficulty of this trip by now, surely those last three sentences from my journal must do it for you. During Student Expedition we were broken into very small groups of just a few individuals, a bit larger for the girls, no instructor with you, and tasked to follow a pre- determined route over extremely difficult terrain, on limited rations, a good part of it far from water)

Tuesday, May 28

Well we had lots to eat and now we're getting ready to take off on our small student groups. I'm paired up with Rob and Big Al, which is really wild since they are…

(Two I will have a hard time getting along with. Rob belonged to some far eastern religion that made him a vegetarian, plus he kept to himself for the most part. Too many Mormons I guess. Big Al complained a lot and had the worst blisters that would have made it into the Guinness Book of World Records)

Oh well, it should only be for 4 days maximum if we don't get lost. We got cheese today for the first time. That's wild. Last night we had fireside and discussed the benefits of the 30 mile hike, (I think that refers to the forced march of a couple days ago) and the run-in. (the last event of the entire trip was to run into the town of Escalante Utah and the bus home)

Well needless to say, some of the ones who were sick and miserable, couldn't see any good in it. There were only about 3. Everyone suffered and all the rest benefited and even enjoyed it, suffering and all.

(Now the 3 of us are off on our own)

Covered about 8 or 9 miles and had supper. Had ash cakes with TVP, cheese, onion and hot sauce inside. Wow! (My mouth is actually watering again over this) Really good… also had potato and onion soup and milk. Now we'll walk until nearly dark and have to dry camp and look for water tomorrow.

Wednesday, May 29

A little cool last night but not too bad. We're in the mouth (actually top) of Silver Falls Canyon heading down to the Escalante River. (where Harris Wash flows in) What a crew! We get along all right but Rob is so particular about preparing his food that it's a mess for Alan and I. Alan just slaps it together and throws it down. I'm somewhere in between. Alan has terrible blisters which slows us down.

(It was amazing that he could even walk. He would start hiking in the morning before Rob and I so he could get use to the pain before Rob and I caught up to him)

We reached the Escalante River and rested for about 2 hours and then went about 5 or 6 miles up it. We're all weak from hunger and it's really a drag. Now we're having trouble with our fire.

(It should be noted that all fires are started the old fashioned way. I use a bow drill that I carried with me for the whole trip. It is reliable but uses a lot of energy starting one, but a fire is so important psychologically as well as for warmth and cooking)

Thursday, May 30

*Cherry & Blueberry filled ash cakes

*Warm milk with cinnamon and Brown Sugar

Hope to get the rest of the way today, close enough so we won't have far to go Friday. But we have the hard part today.

(This was a very difficult day so I quit writing in my journal for a while. This is where we left the river canyon, following the route marked on the topo map, and moved Northeast up 'Horse Canyon', and then up on a bench called Hell's Kitchen I believe. It was nothing but sand and Junipers on top so we dry camped. We were very dehydrated and I was worried that we might have a difficult time getting down off the mesa into 'The Gulch' on the North side where we should find water. Will probably be at least 24 hours between drinking our last water and finding a new source along the way)

Friday, May 31

Started out today without water, were very weak and not sure exactly where we were. (We knew we were on Hell's Kitchen Mesa, but the map showed very steep cliffs where we needed to get down off the mesa) We were walking and I was worrying so I prayed to myself. Within a few minutes we were in a canyon with water and cattails which Rob and I ate. Al is kinda fussy about wild food … and everything else.

(We found an animal trail that wound its way down the cliffs. Outside of animal protein, cattails are about as good as it gets. Grab the stem and pull it out of its root, and you have a starchy stem base fairly high in calories. Bull Rushes are similar but the Utah varieties are very small. The other main wild foods I ate whenever I could find them were flowers of both Yucca and Milkweed – the non-poisonous variety. There were others but these 4 were the most common out there)

We got to our third marker in 'The Gulch' (a wash with water that led into the Escalante) and ate breakfast and lunch combined. Rob and I really chowed down. We've got about 10 miles left to base camp I believe, and it's about 12 or 1 PM, so we should get in tonight.

Saturday, June 1

('Solo' is the last leg of our journey before the 'run- in' to the bus. It's where we are spread out along the Escalante, separated by a couple hundred yards or so and we're supposed to avoid contact with other

Survivor members. A time for reflection, meditation, reading and whatever else)

I'm on 'solo' now so I can catch up on this. We had a terribly hard time picking up the canyon. (Getting off the Mesa we needed to take us into 'The Gulch' and water) We were thirsty and dehydrated and I was getting a little worried. We went down one place and came to a dead end and had to climb out. Finally after really searching, I started praying to myself as I've been doing now quite a lot. We found our canyon and made it to the water and The Gulch in about 10 minutes. In The Gulch, we met Sherry's group. They all had Montezuma and Sherry had a painful fallen arch. We went out of there cross-country and then down into 'Boulder Creek Canyon'. What a pain that place was to get down. Some girls had to swim down part of it (steep cliffs and deep water) but I was determined not to get everything wet so I led the three of us around the deep water with a little rock climbing.

We finally reached the Escalante again after the same old story, asking ourselves, "when will we get there, Just around the next bend?" We made it into base camp just before complete dark. Got our food and spent a cold night sleeping. This morning we got up, I had no breakfast, and went rappelling. Got that waste of energy out of the way, and our instructor took us back down the river ½ mile and put us in our solo spots.

(Everything we did was in conjunction with the formula, 'calories in vs calories out'. You get to the point very early on where you realize your body is slowly wasting away and the only thing you can do about it is to slow that process down some by limiting your movement to the bare essentials. Hiking uphill to rappel down a cliff, something I had done many times in the past when I was much healthier, just didn't compute)

My nearest neighbor is about 300 yards away across the river… Rob.

(The river is only a few yards across and a couple feet deep at most. But it's clean looking, sweet to be near, and feels great on your tired, abused feet. The canyon is about 50 yards across in most places, and sheltered by red sandstone cliffs)

I've got my camp set up among some large Cottonwoods with plenty of firewood all over. Glad I got this spot. Now I get to spend the rest of today and 3 more days here by myself, reading, writing, thinking, and fixing meals and campsite like I was going to stay for a while.

*Have tried besides the usual brown sugar and cinnamon filled ash cakes, putting raisins and oatmeal in with it. Couldn't really tell any difference, but will experiment further when I get home, also with jelly and/or peanut butter in them.

(At this point I should explain the relationship that the BYU Survivalist develops with ash cakes. They are a holy food, something akin to turkey at Thanksgiving, dates and olives to Middle Easterners, or wine to the French and Italians. They become closer than a lover, and more important when on Survival. They demand that you think of them often… and you do. I'm not sure how many of us went home and couldn't wait to share our ash cakes with friends and family, but I'm certain most did… I certainly did. Ash cakes, you helped me survive, you pulled me through a difficult time, I was married to you and I adored you. Plain or folded over to hold in your contents of TVP, Cheese, brown sugar, raisins, and all the other things we could only dream about that we would try once within range of a grocery store… thank you)

Well I decided to get busy and do something constructive. I felt I had gained a lot of strength back, so I got busy building a lean-to. It took me about 3 hours, made out of large strips of cotton wood inner and outer bark. Wind proof, and I hope water proof for a while. I gathered a large pile of firewood and water, ate and arranged everything in the right place. I've still got 1 ½ hours of light… well 1 day down anyway.

Sunday, June 2

Had about an average night's sleep, I let the fire get low, and toward late night and morning, it got cold. None of my clothes will fit me when I get home. That's gonna be a hassle.

A group from Michigan State and Central Michigan just came by, about 15 of them – backpackers. One guy told me that Central is a good Outdoor Education school.

It's about 7 PM now and I feel pretty good. Not that I was cut out to be a hermit, but I've gotten a lot accomplished. Slept late, cooled my feet in the river, written in this journal. Then I decided to get down to business. I've got a Book of Mormon but all of 1st Nephi is missing, so I'm starting with 2nd Nephi and got to chapter 20 so far today. Then I ate a good stew I made up and had cheese, and honey, and brown sugar ash cakes. Man, I'm addicted to them.

Then it started clouding over again like yesterday, and I was reminded of something I was thinking of doing… build a fireplace. I did out of flat sandstone blocks. The top one that keeps the rain out weighs about 90-100 lbs. It also directs the heat into me under the lean-to better. Also put a few more pieces on the lean-to and that's about it.

They didn't give us much food again for these 4 days, so my walking action is kept at a minimum to save energy. It's really a mess always being weak from lack of nutrition but then it helps to appreiate the millions in the world that live and die in that condition.

Monday, June 3

Had a good night's sleep, mainly because it was pretty warm. But I really had to burn a lot of wood to keep it going. Don't want to go through the hassle of starting one from scratch again. Got up late again which helps the time move along. Today should be the hardest. Got everything done I'm going to do except read and gather more wood. Tomorrow won't be so bad because it's the last day and I'll be visited by an instructor . Then I can go in anytime I want Wednesday morning.

Well I slept a little, wrote a little and read a lot, collected firewood and thought. That's the agenda for tomorrow too I guess. Will be another warm night probably – clouded over.

(After a while you really become part of nature out here in some ways. At first, when you feel an ant in your pants or run across your chest under your shirt, you jump around and holler, trying your best to smash or evict the intruder. Lately when that frequent event transpires, you just lay there and let him go or gently help him find his way out… no big deal)

Tuesday, June 4

Had the warmest night ever, didn't even use my blanket until it started getting light out. It sure is a pain waking up just about once an hour to put on more wood to keep the fire going. Then every time I go back to sleep, I switch to a different dream. Well this is my last solo day and night, and besides the run-in of 12 miles to the town of Escalante, I'm home and can't wait. I mention the run-in because the way I feel right now, I couldn't run a mile even if I had to. (Even for ash cakes)

I just had my first bowel movement in 6 days. Seems like just about everyone is having trouble like that, either everything runs through or it's plugged up. It's the food I;m sure, no fruits and vegetables, just grain. Oh yeah, one carrot, potato, onion a week too! Wow!

Just had my visit from Chuck, the head honcho. (instructor) Really a nice guy. Had a talk about improvement of self and the program.

Wednesday, June 5

Really a warm night. Destroyed camp and trucked into base camp. Sat around and then had a testimony meeting, and now we're eating. Having homemade bread with grape jelly. Next we'll have Campbell's Soup, then oatmeal. Stuffed myself so much I thought my stomach would rupture. Actually couldn't move for about 5 minutes. Everyone slept together tonight.

Thursday, June 6

Run-in – ran for about a mile and a half uphill, then had to walk-run alternate. Caught up to Sherry, girls started first, and decided to walk the rest, about 5 miles and forget the running. Running on asphalt after 28 days on dirt and sand, shook my bones apart. What pain. Came into town of Escalante and raided the store. Weighed myself – lost 20 lbs. Bus ride home.

(I started the trip at 163 lbs, finishing at 143. That's a loss of 5 lbs a week on an already slim dude. The first thing I craved most was peanut butter.

After a week of recuperation I found that while hiking straight up the steep mountains east of Provo, I could keep a constant steady pace without the need to rest. We were in super shape.

Sometime after returning home, we had a reunion. While there I heard one of the guys tell several others that while on the 26 mile midnight hike, he was lucky to have found a cherished 'Cherry Flavored Lip Saver' that someone must have dropped along the way! What luck.

LITERATURE ON WILDERNESS THERAPY, OUTDOOR THERAPY, AND ADVENTURE THERAPY

As I started to compile a list that was complete, of various books, articles, research papers, theses and dissertations that dealt with wilderness therapy, I found that there were hundreds available. The scope of that subject alone is more than I wanted to initiate for the purposes of this book. That alone would take a book of it's own. And frankly, a book would be outdated as soon as it was published.

So, let me recommend just a few books here, without giving a book report, and offer some search terms that can be used to browse the Internet.

Adventure Therapy: Theory, Research, and Practice

Gass, Michael

Gillis, H. L. "Lee"

Russell, Keith C.

Shouting at the Sky: Troubled Teens and the Promise of the Wild

Ferguson, Gary

Effective Leadership in Adventure Programming

Priest, Simon

Gass, Michael A.

Wilderness Therapy: Foundations, Theory and Research

Berman, Dene S.

Wilderness Therapy for Women

Cole, Ellen

The Promise of Wilderness Therapy: A Comprehensive Guid to How and Why Wilderness Therapy Can Be a Solution for At-risk Youth Who Aren't Making Headway in Traditional Therapy

Davis-Berman, Jennifer

Berman, Dene

Stories From the Field: A History of Wilderness Therapy

White, Will

Search Terms:

Wilderness Therapy Research

Wilderness Therapy Literature

Adventure Therapy

Outdoor Therapy

LITERATURE ON PRIMITIVE SKILLS (INCLUDING WILDERNESS SURVIVAL)

During the past decade or two, there have been dozens, if not hundreds, of books on primitive skills printed. There is no dearth in knowledge or 'how to' in the printed word today. I devour these books. Or used to. It seems that so many of them are now saying the same thing, and in mostly the same way.

Having said this, there are some great books that I've read and which I would recommend. Be aware that these books are based upon my interests.   At the same time, most of these books I would recommend to any person desiring to have a library in primitive skills (and survival - primitive as well as preparedness survival).

Top Authors:

I've taken the liberty of compiling this list of some of the top authors on wilderness and primitive skills. It is not all-inclusive. But it's a start.

Below this list of authors is a more detailed description of some of the books I have found especially useful.

In no particular order:

Larry Dean Olsen   David Wescott

Cody Lundin

Dave Canterbury

Laurence Gonzales

Ragnar Benson

John 'Lofty' Wiseman

Tom Brown

George W. Sears

Horace Kephart

Nando Parrado

Aron Ralston

Juliane Koepcke

Nicholas Tomihama

Joseph Alton

Creek Stewart

Tom Elpel

Les Stroud

Bradford Angier

John & Geri McPherson

Mors Kochanski

Ellsworth Jaeger

Jon Krakauer

Alfred Lansing

Lauren Elder

Tony Nester

Christopher Nyerges

Tyler White (videos)

Some novel authors include:

Gary Paulsen

Jack London

Jean Craighead George

Some Special Mentions:

***Outdoor Survival Skills* by Larry Dean Olsen**

The book that re-ignited the movement of primitive and wilderness survival skills. Filled with good information, and really, when we're talking primitive skills that predate any book from a printing press, can a book ever be outdated?!

As much for nostalgia as for the information contained in it, this book ought to be on every bookshelf.

***Primitive Technology: A Book of Earth Skills* by David Wescott**

Filled with informative, bite-sized articles about such topics as tanning, knapping, pottery, bow making and basket making, this book is filled with great information. Thanks to Dave for putting together this book, and keeping alive our understanding of primitive ways.

***Primitive Technology II: Ancestral Skill - From the Society of Primitive Technology* by David Wescott**

A continuation of the first volume, this is more of the same.

Well worth the paper it's printed on, and the price you pay from your local bookstore.

Earth Knack: Stone Age Skills for the 21st Century by **Bart Blankenship**

Flintknapping, cordage, hide glue, musical instruments, pottery, pine needle tea, and clothing. Read about what it is and how to do it in this book.

98.6 Degrees: The Art of Keeping Your Ass Alive by **Cody Lundin**

It may be that I'm drawn to the informal and informative style of writing of Cody. But there's a bunch of 'crap' stuff out there on living primitive. NOT in this book, however. I haven't lived like Cody has, for as long or as intensive as he has (since it's his way of life, and more of a 'job' or a 'vacay' for me), but I know what I've experienced, and I know how he writes about it, and how others write about it, and to most other people, it's academic. To Cody, it's life.

And when you're talking life and death stuff, like these survival books do, you want the straight dope. Cody gives it to you. His mindset, and style of sharing this mindset, make this one of the most fun reads in survival that I've had the privilege of coming upon. If you want fluff, this isn't your book. If you want stuff that works, this is it!

When All Hell Breaks Loose: Stuff You Need to Survive When Disaster Strikes by **Cody Lundin**

Marginally applicable to primitive survival skills, but totally applicable to survival in general, this is worth the 20 ounces (or whatever it is) of weight. Worth it's weight in gold? I'd say, yes.

The psych of survival is too often ignored, or brushed over. This, however, is a common theme with Cody, which is what makes his books universally applicable.

***Survival Hacks: Over 200 Ways to Use Everyday Items for Wilderness Survival* by Creek Stewart**

So, Creek Stewart. What appeals to me about Creek is:

- his knowledge

- his willingness to take regular, everyday folks, and help them see that they have what they need to survive

- his humility and teachableness. Just look at his Facebook page to see how he honors what his students teach him! This is the mark of a great teacher, which I feel he is.

- he's a former boy scout, and all around good Christian fellow

The first book that I came across of his was the Unofficial Hunger Games Survival book (see below). I read the title and description, and didn't buy it. I read the author's name, and wondered who needed to take the name of 'Creek' in order to set himself apart to sell books. Then, I picked up this book (Hacks), and found it to be really fun read. Creative. And it got me thinking.

Survival is mostly psychological, with knowledge and skills being huge, yes, but if a person is defeated in his mind, he'll die. Guaranteed. That's what appeals to me about Creek. He gives skills along with an abundance of good faith and hope.

***Build the Perfect Bug Out Survival Skills: Your Guide to Emergency Wilderness Survival* by Creek Stewart**

Now, Creek has written some other 'Perfect' books in this series. They are good. But this one is really good.

I'm personally turned off a bit on the 72-hour bug out bag or survival kit concept. As soon as we put a time limit on an item, and we exceed this time, I believe that we tend to get deflated. And then it's easy to get beat, emotionally.

But any book that Creek puts out is good, FYI. I just like this one the most (of his 'Perfect' series).

***The Unofficial Hunger Games Wilderness Survival Guide* by Creek Stewart**

The title at first threw me off. I didn't know Creek, didn't know his skills, and thought that here was some bum trying to get a quick buck off of the popularity of the movies.

I was wrong.

This is filled with really interesting, practical stuff. Using the movie as a jumping off point for various topics, Creek takes us on a fun and informative survival skill journey that is very useful.

Boy Scouts of America Handbook

Scouting used to be all about nature, outdoors, skills. Plus more great stuff. Lord Baden Powell did a great thing for the youth of the world by birthing the scouting movement.

***Bushcraft 101: A Field Guide to the Art of Wilderness Survival* by
Dave Canterbury**

I didn't know about Dave until he and Cody were on Dual
Survival. And there, I thought that Cody conquered through finesse and
thought and skill, and Dave conquered through bulk and brawn and
sheer power and muscle.

Reading these books helps me to understand that there's a 'brain
side' to Dave, as well as a brawn side. Filled with good stuff, I wish
that these had been around 30 years ago when I first entered the desert,
and 40 years ago when I first entered the Bob Marshall Wilderness.

***Advanced Bushcraft: An Expert Field Guide to the Art of Wilderness
Survival* by Dave Canterbury**

Same as above.

Just, good stuff.

***Edible Wild Plants: A North American Field Guide to Over 200
Natural Foods* by Thomas Elias**

The title says it all.

***Survive!: Essential Skills and Tactics to Get You Out of Anywhere -
Alive* by Les Stroud**

Who doesn't need more tactics?

There's more than one way to skin a cat (so, I've skinned a lot of animals - never a cat), and knowing others experiences is so helpful. That's what I like about Les' book.

The Survival Medicine Handbook: A Guide for When Help is Not on the Way by Joseph Alton, MD

I like when the 'experts' show us that we can do some of the things that they can do. When it all hits the fan, and a doc isn't around, I'm still going to do something to save my loved ones. In this book, Dr. Alton knows this, and shows us how to maximize the chance that we will do the right thing.

There are some other books that he and his wife have also written, and a podcast I've listened to before. I highly recommend them.

Bushcraft: Outdoor Skills and Wilderness Survival by Mors Kochanski

Our friend to the North, Mors Kochanski has helped to spread the word on all sorts of crafts: Axcraft, knifecraft, sheltercraft, bushcraft. A living legend, one of the wise ones, Mors has some great advice and teachings in this book.

Desert Solitaire by Edward Abbey

Please, don't all of my conservative friends freak out that this is in here. And please don't all of my bushcraft friends freak out that this is in here. And please don't all of my tree-hugging friends get excited about this being in here.

There's really nothing survivally about this book. Unless one considers that Abbey wanted to help the desert survive.

So, why is this book here? Because it's, plain and simple, a really, really fun read. Actually, I listened to the book, and the narration that I heard from the words that Abbey wrote was enthralling.

It helps to paint a picture of peace in the desert.

As a disclaimer, I must confess to reading this very week a book by Amy Irvine titled **Desert Cabal**. She takes on the great Abbey, on the fiftieth anniversary of the printing of **Desert Solitaire**. I would also recommend her book, though I'm not done with it.

The banter about the politics of the desert is interesting. But the behind-stories (the background info) about the deserts, is really what's fun. That, and the 'human-ness' of the people trying to ascribe human characteristics to the land. And the relationships. It's all about relationship, eventually.

Epic Survival by Matt Graham

This book, by one of the up and coming (or is he up and on top?) bushcrafter survivalists is a really fun read. With a forward by Dave Wescott, wherein he mentions that some of Matt's experiences are unbelievable, this is almost true. But Dave believes Matt, and so do I.

Matt talks about racing horses, living on dollars a month (or nothing), his struggles between the peace of the solitary life on the land and the native desires, even instincts, to have a relationship to satisfy the higher needs on Maslow's hierarchy.

But always back to the wilderness. A great book wherein Matt is (mostly) transparent, and it is appealing. It's about wilderness, self-deprivation, self-control, limits, achievement, and peace.

ART CREDITS

A big thank you to Kelly Magleby for graciously being willing to contribute photographs for the covers. As I went to put them onto the book, I realized that the resolution was too small, and so couldn't use them. So, you're stuck with my phone photos.

Thank you to my son Enoch, for finding a program that allows me to make photo sketches from the photographs I take. The sketches throughout the book were made from this program *Sketch Photo*. I took the photographs, or rather, I instructed my cell phone to capture the images.

I also need to give my wife Christine credit for some of the photos. Since we are 'one,' I didn't feel the need to point out her photographs. Plus, I'm just getting her back for the year that she put her name on one of my photographic entries in the local county fair, and she came away with a purple ribbon and a trip to the Utah State Fair. ;)

Lastly, but Mostly, I thank my God, the Creator, who gives to me, and each of us, a daily dose of visual reminders that through all of our struggles, there is beauty all around, still.

GLOSSARY

There's nothing scientific or 'approved' about this glossary. The explanations are my own, and didn't go through any committee for approval. I hope that they do clarify, however, how the words are used in this book.

Abo: A practitioner of the aboriginal skills, or what we also call wilderness survival skills.

Young Abo: youth participants in the wilderness survival programs. Most usually in the program involuntarily.

Instructor Abo: Paid participants in wilderness survival programs. Ideally they have their act together, in life, and can not only teach primitive skills such as bow-drill fire, flint-and-steel fire, cordage, traps, etc, but also can model good relationships.

Anasazi: The ancient Native American's who inhabited the Southwestern part of the United States about 1,000 years ago.

Anasazi Foundation: One of the first wilderness survival programs in the country, started by Larry Dean Olsen and Zeke Sanchez.

Ash Cake: Flour mixed with water and then cooked directly on the coals of a fire. A staple food of the program when I was an instructor abo. Always flavored with coals. Sometimes flavored and enhanced with bugs, ants, and plants.

Behavior Modification: Changing the behavior of the young abos.

Belt Buckle Strap: Used as the shoulder straps for our primitive packs. Went around each shoulder then tied at the waist, to also form a waist belt.

Big Spencer Flat: A high desert plain between Escalante and Boulder Utah. One of the few places where moqui marbles can be found.

Boot Camp: The army philosophy of training. Though there are no programs that utilize this philosophy in eliciting change in young abos now, the program that I worked for in the 1980's used this philosophy in their operations.

BOSS: *Boulder Outdoor Survival School*. Started by Doug Nelson in the 1980's. A premier training school for primitive skills in the United States.

Bow-Drill: A primitive method of starting a fire. The component parts are a bow, drill, cordage, a palm rock, fireboard, and a coal.

Brown, Tom: The East Coast guru of wilderness survival.

Burr Trail: Originally a cow trail, this was the dropping off point for many of the young abos in the 1980's, when I worked there.

Bustin' A Coal: The work that it takes to create a hot coal from the dust of wood with a bow-drill is called bustin' a coal.

Cactus Spikes: Found on prickly pear. The spikes would be burned and cut off in order to eat the flesh of the cactus. The spikes were also used by the Young Abos to keep their pierced holes open.

Carmex: It is a lip protector. It was used on our lips, and various other parts of the body, to prevent and treat chapping. When the glass jar was empty, it was used as a palm rock in a bow drill set. One of the best palm rocks I've ever used.

Cat hole: The hole that human excrement was deposited in. Buried after it was lovingly used.

Challenger: *Challenger Foundation*. The company I worked for. Probably the largest at that time.

Chipping Site: The spot where Native American's sat and chipped agate, jasper, and obsidian into arrowheads, knives, etc.

Cliff Dwelling: The homes of the ancient Anasazi and Fremont cultures. Also, our temporary homes.

Coal Bed: A rectangular-shaped hole is dug, approximately 12-18 inches deep (depending on the soil type), being about 12 inches by 24 (and up to 36) inches in shape. Non-porous rocks are placed in the hole, and a fire is built on on the rocks. After burning for an hour or so, the hot rocks are then buried with the soil removed from the hole. This coal bed will keep a person warm throughout the night.

Cognitive Therapy: Talk therapy. Using *reason* to work through problems, and to chart a future course.

Crytogram: A soil that is alive. Organisms live on and in the soil, and stabilize it from wind and rain erosion. When the soil is disturbed by stepping on it, much of the positive impact of the organisms are negated. We tried to avoid stepping on this soil.

Death Ridge: A ridge on the Kaiparowits Plateau that seemed to be seldom-visited, or at least parts of it were seldom visited. It could have been the name that accounted for the vacancies of human beings. This is where I saw a dinosaur bone on top of the ground, sitting on an ancient chipping site.

Desert Solitaire: A book written by former Park Service employee Edward Abbey. It was something that was suggested I read in 1989, but I declined to do so then. In 2018, I listened to it, and found it absolutely amazing in the words that he used. Politically I either really agree with him or disagree with him, but the adventures that he recounts are fun to hear about.

Desert Varnish: Rain and moisture seep out and over the sandstone, taking minerals with them, then, as the water evaporates, the minerals are deposited on the surface of the sandstone, looking like a painting.

Eagle Scout: The highest rank in the Boy Scouts of America. Camping, hiking, and other outdoor activities are required in order to attain this rank. Through the help of some great scout leaders and parents, I obtained this rank.

Escorts: Usually male, but sometimes female, folks who went to a youth's home or town, and brought them back to the program. They 'escorted' the youth to Boulder or Escalante, Utah, to go through the program.

Fire to Fire: A great primitive skills gathering held in Utah, usually the same week as the Summer equinox. Brad Wade started this gathering. An infant *Rabbitstick*.

Frankl, Victor: A German Jew who was imprisoned in the harsh labor camps during WWII. He lost his family. He was a physician and also a psychiatrist. He came up with logotherapy, which is the philosophy that if a person can find a 'why' any 'what' can be endured and learning can occur.

Freedom: The ability to make choices, and to live a life filled with alternatives. We all have freedom to varying degrees. As Frankl points out, even when we are physically restricted, we still have the freedom to chose our thoughts and attitude.

All of us make choices that limit our freedom. What we eat, put into our minds, lack of exercise, etc., all impact our freedoms. Our choices also allow us to have greater freedom. Freedom is, therefore, a direct result of the choices that we make.

Granary: Usually a small room with the front wall constructed using head-sized rocks, with the intent of storing grain for later use.

Head Staff: There were usually three or four staff per group of 9-12 Young Abos. The leader of these 3 or 4 staff was named the head staff.

Hole-in-the-Rock Road: Mormon pioneers forged their way through the harsh environment of southern Utah, down to the Colorado River. They were stopped from going forward by the gorge that the Colorado River flows in. They found a hole in the rock, and lowered their wagons down to the Colorado River.

Kaipairowits Plateau: A higher mountain range overlooking the lower desert. Located south of Escalante. There are chipping site and fossils, including shark teeth, in the rock making up the plateau.

Knife: When a bow-drill fire was made, a knife was one of the rewards. This knife was usually worn around the neck. Sometimes there was a hole burned into the handle, and the knife was also used as a palm rock.

Maslow, Abraham: A psychologist who postulated that in order for a person's higher needs to be met, their lower needs must first be addressed and adequately satisfied. I saw this in some of the students. If a student had a fast metabolism and finished his or her food before the next food drop, they focused on food to the point that no good emotional work was done.

He developed a philosophy that has been given life in a diagram known as *Maslow's Hierarchy of Needs*.

Moqui Marbles: A unique rock found on Big Spencer Flat near Escalante, Utah, and some surrounding areas. They seem to be made of iron, but when broken open, they are filled with a compressed sand.

They are found in shapes of a ball to a UFO shape. We would sometimes use the ones that were shaped right as a palm rock. But until it was worn smooth inside, it would wear down the spindle of our bow-drill set. Some attribute spiritual qualities to the rock.

Naming Ceremony: Each Young Abo would receive a new name, patterned after Native American names, that described their personality traits, and gave them a 'boost' to see themselves in a different way.

Outdoor Behavioral Health Council (OBHC): An organization started by a few outdoor behavioral programs, where membership is voluntary, and intended to self-regulate the treatment programs offered outdoors. This was created to maintain a safe environment for Young Abos, the workers, and to regulate safety issues internally so that external regulation wouldn't become necessary.

Outdoor Survival Skills: 1) The name of the book written by Larry Dean Olsen, that started the primitive skills movement. A must-own for all outdoor and primitive skills enthusiasts.

2) That skill set that is acquired and developed that allows one to survive outdoors, and away from civilization. May or may not be related to *primitive* skills. Instead, outdoor survival skills utilizes whatever is necessary and available at the moment, no matter the origin of the item or article being used.

Outdoor Therapy: Psychotherapy, or counseling, that occurs outside of an office, home, or facility. Typically, the experiences in the outdoors are also utilized as a catalyst for change.

P-51: The army can opener.

Palm Rock: That part of the bow-drill set that is held in the hand, and holds the top, pointed part of the spindle in place.

Paracord: At first utilized in parachuting, but now has numerous uses in an outdoor situation. We used paracord as a bow-drill string, and to tie our tarps, blankets, and items into a backpack-type bundle that we carried on our back.

Paradox: Something that seems counter-intuitive. "The first shall be last, and the last shall be first" is an example. In therapy in the outdoors, there are many paradoxes.

- The best counseling is to be quiet, and observe.

- Absence (of food) makes the heart grow stronger

- The yells often go unheaded, whilst the whispers are those that move

Picadilly: A formed potato bite, similar to fries, but shaped like an inflated postage stamp, deep fried and best eaten with fry sauce.

Pit House: A home or structure made by Native Americans.

Poncho: The army-issue poncho that we used had a hood, were rectangular, and snapped together to form the outer shell in which was placed our wool blanket, which we used as a sleeping bag.

Prickly Pear Cactus: A cactus with sharp spines, both long and short, that was edible. We ate cactus about every other day. The large spines were cut off. The 'hair-like' spines were often burned off in a bed of coals. The large spines would hurt for a few moments if they pricked us, but it is the small spines that would irritate us for hours or days.

For variety, nothing beat the Prickly Pear!

Primitive Survival Skills: Those skills acquired and practiced which used no modern implement, but just what could be found in the wilds. This even included not using a man-made knife, but only using those items which we could find in the wilds, naturally.

Rabbitstick: The premier gathering for practitioners of primitive skills, survival skills, and old-time camping skills. Held annually in September near Rexburg, Idaho. Started by Larry Dean Olsen, but carried on now by David Wescott. The attendees include THE 'Who's Who' A-list of current skill practitioners.

Run-In: Students would 'run in' to their parents near the end of their outdoor experience. At run-in, they would have successfully completed their program, be reunited with their family, and would spend the next few days teaching their parents some of the skills that they learned, primitive as well as relationship skills.

Sections

Impact: The initial section of the program, lasting only a few days to a few weeks, where the students were not-so-gently eased into their new living situation.

Primitive Survival: The first 21 days of the program, where the students were taught the beginnings, the basics, of survival in the wilderness. Many of the fires were made for them, but they learned to forage, to adapt and improvise, and to take a hard look at their life prior to the program.

Advance Survival: The next 21 days of the program, where some more advanced concepts of survival were taught, and the skills initiated during Primitive Survival were practiced even more. Traps, cordage, pottery, foraging, fire-making, navigation, shelters, water-procurement - all of these were taught and practiced.

Handcarts: One may say this last 21-day section was more easy, but I would disagree. The terrain was such that handcarts were used. So it wasn't as rough. However, it was mileage-intensive. The food was better, and dutch ovens were used. Fire-making wasn't an issue anymore, since the Young Abos already knew how to make a fire using both a bow-drill as well as flint and steel.

Sheep Kill: Typically, once during the 63+ day program, a sheep (or more than one) was brought in to camp, they youth were taught how to process every part of the sheep, and a feast was had for a few days.

It's interesting that Oliver North flew in to one of the sheep kills during the time I was employed by the program. I was gone at the time, but I understand that he and the owner of the program were friends.

Skinny Runners: The ancient 'spirit people' of the desert. Standing sideways, they were unnoticeable. They could come into your camp and spirit some of your items away. There were some honorable Skinny Runners and some dishonorable ones. They were fast, but if they so choose, some humans would be allowed to glimpse them. They did not converse with us.

Solo: A period of one to three nights that the students spent in their own camp, in a shelter of their own making, reflecting upon the life that they would create when they went home. Had a counselor been present to help them to clarify some of their future ambitions, and learn how to use some of their past issues to catapult them forward, Solo would have been much more useful.

Survival Skills: Any skill that is needed to survive is known as a survival skill. Many of these students were experts at surviving in their home environments, that may have been less than stellar. Rich or poor, most had a home, school, or social life that was a struggle in some way.

In the wilderness, they could adapt the lessons they had learned to survive at home, into their present environment. When they did this, they fared well in the program. They then came to understand how they could use the skills they had developed in positive ways.

Traps: There were three primary traps that were taught to the Young Abos, and which they used to procure additional protein (food). These were the Figure Four, Paiute Deadfall, and the Snare.

Snakes were the primary food, though the traps also brought birds, a few squirrels, and many insects to our 'table.'

Wescott, Dave: Took over BOSS from Doug Nelson. Taught at BYU-Idaho for decades, and re-initiated Rabbitstick.

Wilderness Therapy: This has been re-branded as behavioral healthcare in the outdoors. Basically, wilderness therapy is the roughest and most basic of all outdoor behavioral healthcare philosophies. The goal is to encourage both a change of heart as well as change of behavior by using primitive and survival skills as a catalyst.

Wool Blanket: This army-issue blanket, made of wool of course, was our sleeping bag, along with a poncho, for the entire summer.

WYSIWYG: Probably an extremely outdated term, as I learned it in high school. But still, a very useful term. What You See Is What You Get. Computer monitors used to show something different on the screen than was printed. They were not WYSIWYG.

People are like this in many ways. Society tends to reward those who are in public acceptable and admirable, no matter what their personal life is. So, most people learn that WYSIWYG is not rewarded. *Fake* is the opposite of WYSIWYG.

People

Young Abos (trees)

    Tall Aspen

Wandering Juniper

Rocking Pine

Straight Oak

Laughing Woodchip

Bending Ash

Blue Juniper

Winding Branch

Happy Sage

Instructor Abos (rocks)

Flying Gypsum

Walking Agate

Kneeling Jasper

Chipped Obsidian

A chapter in my book *Ruminations From the Burr Trail.*

Boulder Mountain

We arrived at Boulder Mountain, the first lookout, about 2:23 PM. Time-stamped from the photograph on my phone camera. f/2.0; 1/1783 shutter speed; 3.56 mm; ISO 50. Go figure! Technology.

I've stopped here before, by myself occasionally, but mostly with my family. I can think of twice before when my three sons and I stopped here. And I've got photos from each time. It's a fun look-out spot. It's on a mountain, in a mountainous, treeish, greenish-type of spot. Aspens and pines fill the area. But then one can look and see, in the far distance, the Henry mountains - lacolithic mountains - with tops dusted with snow. Actually, probably more than dusted, since it can be seen dozens of miles away.

And between the Henry's and the Boulder (the mountain where we are), is Capitol Reef National Park, the Escalante / Grand Staircase National Monument, and Butch Cassidy country. And blue sky. With white clouds. A big sky. A real big sky. I'm from Montana, and know big sky, but this rivals the hugeness of the Montana sky.

As happens each time we stop here, my boys run and jump from boulder to boulder. They stop and look at the distant mountains, the seemingly waterless landscape of the Navajo sandstone country, and the big sky, but only for seconds, literally. Then they're back to their jumping and running. But that's OK. I hope that the imprint of this moment, and their brief glances at the landscape, will come back to them some decade in the future. Their memory, prompted by the photographs that I take, will hopefully also bring back the good feelings that they are experiencing now. And maybe they'll remember this trip that their old man took 'em on. To where he worked nearly 30 years ago.

A Snapshot in Time

To more fully remember this moment, at least sometime in the future, I call my sons to my side, and ask them to face away from the grand scenery whilst I hand my phone / camera to a lady whom I've asked to take our picture. She is a traveller, with her travelling male companion. The travel-van types. But nice. And smiley.

And so, with a huge smile on her face, she is extremely accommodating. We line up, face her, she faces the scenery, puts us the middle of the digital screen, and tells us to smile.

Then she notices that one of my sons is standing with his arms at his side, whilst the rest of us have our arms around each others back. She directs this son, Enoch, to do the same. "*You (need to) look like you like each other*," she tells him in her foreign accent. And he obeys her, even more quickly than he obeys his mother (though he really is a good kid).

She then zooms out (or in) and takes another photo for good measure. Then hands my phone back to me. I don't think to even look at the pictures until later that afternoon. When I see them, I like them. In one there is a lot of scenery in the background, and the other, of course, is filled with my 220 pounds of proud fatherhood, with three of my sons!

Enoch looks at the photo too, and I make some comment which leads him to tell me that the gal who took the photographs said that she is a photographer. I then look at these with new eyes, and think, "Yup, they are good." Truthfully, probably no better than any other snapshot from our trip, but still, fun stuff.

In retrospect, most of the fun of the photo is the memories - the real memories of the moment, and the memories I hope to have ten years from now when I look at this photo again.

Their patience used up with the fifteen seconds worth of photographs, the boys are back to bounding and bouncing around the boulders on Boulder Mountain. This is a fun place, even though we've been here three times.

Preceding Stopovers

The last time, about 14 months ago, was when we came with another fellow and his son. We stayed in a our teepee tent in the National Park. One day we drove over the Boulder to the other side, and hiked to a place known as Lower Calf Creek Falls. It's an easy hike, but filled with people.

"Filled" is a relative term, mind you. We probably did see a hundred folks on the trail that day, but when the hope is to see nobody, 100 people is allot.

The time before last, our first time in the area, was when these same three sons and I hiked to Lower Calf Creek Falls, and also stayed in the campground there. We had a tent, but it was warm enough to sleep on top of it. We wanted to see the sky, and there weren't that many people, so our space didn't seem too violated. We layed our tent out, and just put our sleeping bags on top. That was after our hike to the falls, six miles round trip, and after being dive-bombed by bats on our hike back at dusk.

I don't know if they were going for *us*, if we had *bugs* around around us that they were going for, or if we were just *bugging them*. But whatever the cause, the bats were, literally, coming at us; flying straight down towards us, then at the last micro-second, swooping upwards. We laughed, but inwardly I was getting scared. Not of the bats, but of the rabies that I heard that bats carry.

At any rate, this, the third time on the Boulder, in this same spot, was the most fun.

Bustling Boulder Town

After a few more minutes of running, jumping, and generally disturbing the peace of the natural inhabitants of the area, as well as some of the gnarly cranky elderly tourists, we left. Heading South again, it wasn't too long before we entered the city limits of Boulder.

Again, city is a relative term. And I actually think that Boulder may be, technically, a town. Population determines that, I believe. Not size, for sure, since we passed the Boulder city limit sign about three miles before we actually hit city center! And if there was even one house in that span of distance, I don't remember it. Maybe they claim the wildlife on their census as part of their numbers, and thus are able to get more federal funding?! Hmmm - I don't know.

We were about to the town center when, off to our left was an old, worn out, broken down rodeo grounds. I didn't see any grandstands, but there was an old announcers booth. One that surely could not be insured! The next big wind will take it down, I'm afraid.

But it was so neat to see that I set my right foot to the brake and stopped in the middle of the road. Backing up about 30 yards took me to where I wanted to be to capture a photograph of the place. Still in the middle of the road, I pulled out my trusty Moto phone and took still another snapshot (on this trip, not this place).

My sons are used to me now, and mostly they just glance around, then go back to their phones or reading the insides of their eyelids. However, one son glances back, through the rear window, hoping that I didn't choose the time to stop during the once-every-five-minutes when a car comes along the road.

Luck was with us. No cars, so we're safe.

I get the photo, and according to some abo traditions, take a part of the soul with me. Then head on down the road.

And I think to myself, "I don't want to take anything away from here but good memories." And I then think, "I believe that I add soul to this place, add energy, by giving it the extra thought, rather than just driving by. A photograph will help me recall with fondness what I'm feeling now."

No - photographs build a place, a person, rather than detract from them. (Except with pornography.)

Reminiscences of By-Gone Decades

As we enter the town, my mind is flooded with memories:

Twenty nine years ago, plus a few months, I first entered Boulder, Utah, in my little red / orange 1976 Toyota Corolla hatchback.

This car, and the contents, fit the image of who I would become. Filled with most of my physical possessions, transporting a bandanna-wearing skinny 23-year old who was about to find out what desert life was really like. I came to work in a wilderness survival program (most are now known as outdoor adventure programs). I'd never been to Boulder, and never had really been to the high desert before.

The company I worked for rented an A-frame house on the south end of town. The only furniture that I recall - a peeling table and some rickety chairs. Mostly filled with army ponchos, wool blankets, rice and lentils, this house was 'base camp' for the program. During the next week of my life, I would be in and out of Boulder.

We never slept in the house itself, but always outside. We were, after all, a wilderness program. So why ruin things by sleeping in a building.

We visited what must have been the main office of BOSS, or Boulder Outdoor Survival School. Richard, the fellow employed by the program to train new field staff, went by a yurt-type structure a few times during training. Richard was connected with BOSS in some way.

Then, my memories tumbled forward in time, to two years ago, when my sons and I were in the town on a respite from our stay at Calf Creek Falls Campground. We were filling our water bottles up with potable water and emptying our bladders of our used-up water at a local park / playground area, when a motley crew of people, stinky just like us, and dressed just like us (they'd been in the outback) took up temporary residence in the park, just like us. I told my boys that these folks must be BOSS participants. It was fun to just sit back in the shade and watch them.

Then I thought of present-day Boulder. This town is frequented by such outdoor survival icons as David Holliday and Matt Graham. Legend and up-and-coming Legend, they both have lived near Boulder, and have walked the same streets that we were driving on. Cody Lundin too, of *Dual Survival* fame, started his outdoor path here in this area, I understand. And possibly about the same time that I roamed these streets and the Burr Trail with Richard.

Would someday one of my sons be in this same category, I wondered? Would they someday be one of the new outdoor survivors, a primitive specialist who was a folk hero for a day? Would people speak of David Holliday, Matt Graham, Cody Lundin, and ... (fill in the blank) Dye? My son!

No, I thought. They don't seem to be of that temperament or desire. They're here now out of respect for me, and not so much because this is their first (or in their top five) choice of activities.

I was determined, however, to make our trip a positive and memorable one.

From Wild Desert to National Monument

We stopped at the small gas station in town and filled up with gas. I wanted a full tank prior to heading out on the Burr Trail. One never knew when a full tank would be needed! I remembered a gas station on the very south edge of town, but it was larger, and more of a convenience store. The place I stopped was in the middle of town, a bit run down, and nostalgic. A mom and pop place. A dying breed in rural America. I want to give my money, or the credit card's money, to this place. Maybe it will stay in business one more day because of my purchase. When something like this dies, a part of America dies too. That causes me to be sad.

We pass by the Anasazi State Park office, that also has a sign saying that there is information on the Escalante / Grand Staircase National Monument inside as well. I *do* hesitate just a little. Always one to want to go just a little deeper than surface level, I think that we could find out more about the land we were going to visit.

Years ago, when I last drove the Burr Trail, it was wild. It was remote. It was impassible during and after a rainstorm. But now, I didn't know what to expect. Because we were heading into a monument -- an officially branded and legal and set-apart National Monument. This was new stuff to me, and I wasn't sure what else was new. So, I admit, I considered stopping in at the information center.

But then I think, "Is the kind of stuff we want to learn on this trip found in there?" The answer - no. What I want, and what I want my boys to want, can't be found at the visitor's center. So, we head south from the gas station, and turn left, following the directions on the signs.

We're on the Burr Trail!

Look for this book, and others, on Amazon.

And follow me on my Facebook page: Author David Dye

To get a list of the ten most common primitive skills and ten greatest psychological skills the Young Abos learned in the program, send an email to me at *epochadventure@gmail.com*.

This will also put you on my mailing list, to be notified of upcoming publications, primitive skills events, trainings, etc. Being a therapist, I understand the nature of confidentiality, and will not send, or give away, your email address and other information.